FOREWORD BY **JOHN C. MAXWELL**

Impact the World

LIVE YOUR VALUES AND DRIVE CHANGE AS A
CITIZEN STATESPERSON

CARRIE RICH · DEAN FEALK

WILEY

Published by John Wiley & Sons, Inc., Hoboken, New Jersey.
Published simultaneously in Canada.

For general information on our other products and services or for technical support, please contact our Customer Care Department within the United States at (800) 762-2974, outside the United States at (317) 572-3993 or fax (317) 572-4002.

Wiley also publishes its books in a variety of electronic formats. Some content that appears in print may not be available in electronic formats. For more information about Wiley products, visit our web site at www.wiley.com.

Library of Congress Cataloging-in-Publication Data

Names: Rich, Carrie, author. | Fealk, Dean, author. | John Wiley & Sons, publisher.
Title: Impact the world : live your values and drive change as a citizen statesperson / Carrie Rich, Dean Fealk.
Description: Hoboken, New Jersey : Wiley, [2022] | Includes index.
Identifiers: LCCN 2021062495 (print) | LCCN 2021062496 (ebook) | ISBN 9781119848912 (cloth) | ISBN 9781119848936 (adobe pdf) | ISBN 9781119848929 (epub)
Subjects: LCSH: Social change—Citizen participation. | Political planning—Citizen participation.
Classification: LCC HM831 .R53 2022 (print) | LCC HM831 (ebook) | DDC 303.4—dc23/eng/20220301
LC record available at https://lccn.loc.gov/2021062495
LC ebook record available at https://lccn.loc.gov/2021062496

Cover Image: © Bryan Blanchard
Cover Design: Wiley

SKY10033158_031622

Carrie's Dedication: To Hayden David, Lily Isannah, Benjamin Monte, and Darren, you already impact my world.

Dean's Dedication: To Ellie, Elyse and Anders for lighting the way as my North Star.

Contents

Foreword

OVER THE COURSE of my career, I have met countless people who think leadership is only a noun; that a "leader" is simply something you are, based on your place in an organization. These individuals are at the pinnacle of government, industry, and nonprofit organizations. They have titles that mark them out as a manager, a director, a supervisor, or an executive. They view their place in the world as static—as a "leader" who is in charge of people or processes or operations.

But here's the truth: that's not what leadership is. Leadership isn't about a role or a title, and just because someone is designated as a leader doesn't mean they are one. Instead, leadership is active; it's vigorous and dynamic and energetic. It's not limited to people in high-ranking positions, or restricted to those with money or power. Instead, it's available to all people with character and determination—and it is deeply, deeply necessary.

From poverty and homelessness to violence and corruption, we often see challenges in the world around us and ask, "Why doesn't someone do something?" We look to people with more experience, or people with more influence, or people with more time or resources than ourselves to step up and find answers to some of our biggest problems. But what if we didn't wait for others? What if we stepped up, and looked for ways to employ our skills in order to solve the biggest and most complex problems of our time?

That's what leaders do.

When I first met Dean and Carrie years ago, it was clear that they were leaders. Dean had already broken barriers in the private sector and foreign policy through his unwavering determination and incredible talent, forging a remarkable career in law and international diplomacy and developing a reputation for insight and perseverance. Carrie had built an impressive legacy in social action through her own personal magnetism and go-getting style; after trying to raise $6,000 to help six organizations, Carrie ended up being given not one million but two million dollars—and turned that success into The Global Good Fund, which helps social entrepreneurs all over the world.

Carrie and Dean are living examples that leadership isn't just about being at the top of your game, but rather about bringing others up to amplify their impact. After all, there's no doubt that the authors of this book possess the qualities to be personally successful. They are grounded, with the kind of authenticity and integrity that keeps them focused on their values. They are gifted, with natural skills that help them succeed in the service of others. They are constantly growing, with an unending desire to learn, improve, and expand their impact. They show from their incredible stories that you don't need to begin with power and money and influence to leave a positive mark on the world, and that true leadership isn't only about who we are, but what we do.

What makes Carrie and Dean so special is they don't just advocate for leadership; they live it. It emanates from them, transforming the people around them. It expands to connect with others, creating a larger force for good in the world. Through their work, Carrie and Dean are committed to making change at scale by sharing their own understanding and expertise and helping others realize their potential as changemakers, trailblazers, and citizen statespeople.

That's why this isn't just a book about leadership—it's a book about how to become a citizen statesperson. Through examples and exercises and discussion, Dean and Carrie take you on a journey that will help you ignite your spark of leadership, build your network and your expertise, and leverage your skills and resources to change the world. In the pages that follow, Carrie and Dean show not only how they were able to make their extraordinary impact, but how you can make yours. They encourage you to maximize your potential. They inspire you to find better ways to serve your community, your country, and your world. And they teach you how to take the concrete steps necessary to turn ideas into action.

I hope that you find this book as exciting as I do. I know you will be as grateful for Dean and Carrie's example and wisdom as I am. And I am certain that, with this book in hand, you will continue to do everything in your power to make a difference—by doing something that makes a difference, with people who make a difference, at a time that makes a difference.

You're in good hands—and I can't wait to see what you do next.

John C. Maxwell

Acknowledgments

THIS BOOK WAS Dean's idea. He jokingly suggested that we write this book together and I seriously answered that any excuse to have routine exposure to Dean's perspective and humor was reason enough for me. Dean, most people describe the process of writing a book as a great challenge and at times painstaking; you made this project fun.

Thank you to the Eisenhower Foundation for gifting me the experience of a lifetime as an Eisenhower Fellow, and for introducing me to Dean and many other citizen statespeople.

To The Global Good Fund Fellows, you made me want to write this book because it is an honor to showcase your meaningful work. Your drive to impact the world inspires me.

To The Global Good Fund team, board, and community, thank you for your support. You consistently encourage me to share my story in the context of making the world a better place.

To John Wiley & Sons, publishers, thank you for giving us a chance.

To my family, biological and chosen, you know who you are. I love you.

To aspiring citizen statespeople, you know who you are. I believe in you.

****

Carrie - You are a leader among leaders who never fails to bring out the best in all of us. Thank you for standing steadfastly alongside me on this project. Our work has just begun.

My unwavering gratitude to the teachers and mentors who lift us high upon their wings.

To the citizen statespeople: may you always find the courage within to step forward alone; but rest assured that we are always behind you.

Why Being a Citizen Statesperson Matters

> **Key Takeaways**
>
> - A citizen statesperson is a superpowered individual committed to improving the community and the world through values and activism.
> - Three dynamics drive the need and opportunity for citizen statespeople at this moment: 1) loss of confidence in traditional institutions of power and influence, 2) technology that contributes to the capability of the superpowered individual, and 3) a new generation of impact-minded individuals committed to driving change in meaningful and multifaceted ways.
> - Becoming a citizen statesperson starts at a local level, solving problems for local people. From there, citizen statespeople can make a global impact.

ABBEY WEMIMO WAS born in Nigeria and grew up in the slums of Lagos. He lost his father when he was two years old, and was raised by his mother and two sisters. Even as a child, he understood that his circumstances meant that he wouldn't be able to access everything he needed in life, and that his experience would prove challenging and at times disappointing. He was also a smart and motivated child, and his mother believed fundamentally in the importance of a good education. Excluded from the traditional financial system, Abbey's mother turned to rotational savings to pay for food and his school fees, and sent her son to one of the finest high schools in Nigeria. He took international exams to qualify for universities abroad, and at 17 years old, he was offered a once-unimaginable opportunity: an education in the United States.

He and his mother emigrated together to Minnesota, but when they arrived, they struggled to survive. They tried to borrow money for Abbey's college tuition from one of the largest banks in Minneapolis, but the bank turned them away because they lacked a credit score or a financial history. Ultimately, in order to send Abbey to college, his mother was forced to pawn her wedding ring and borrow a few thousand dollars from a predatory lender at an interest rate of over 400 percent.

The experience had a profound impact on Abbey. He turned down an opportunity to play professional soccer, and instead focused on gaining an education in business and finding jobs in the financial sector, determined to learn about the system that had nearly destroyed his family and so many others across the United States. Along the way, he looked for opportunities to connect with leaders and innovators who were working to improve communities around the world.

Eventually, that work brought him to Samir Goel.

Samir's parents traveled from New Delhi, India, in search of a better life through the American Dream, but when they arrived in America, they quickly faced a colder and more challenging reality than they had anticipated. On their first day in the United States, Samir's father was robbed by a mugger, who took what little money he had brought with him. The place they had intended to stay was no longer able to shelter them. With no money, no credit score, and nowhere to live, Samir's parents struggled to survive—a beginning that forced them to "work miracles," as Samir puts it, to give him the future that they imagined.

Samir took their experience to heart and worked hard to secure a good education and a career that could sustain him and his family. Samir simultaneously looked for ways to serve communities that had been left out and left behind. He gained experience in start-ups and social impact ventures, and connected with other young people who were determined to make a contribution to the world around them.

Though Abbey and Samir came from different communities, they learned the same lesson: that for people without a financial history—especially people of color—opportunities for advancement can be scarce. They saw beyond their parents' experiences to the millions of men, women, and children who were dogged by the same challenge. And when they met at the Clinton Global Initiative in 2014, they pledged to do something about it.

For a few years, they continued to work in corporate roles—Abbey at Goldman Sachs and PricewaterhouseCoopers, and Samir at LinkedIn—but they kept discussing their families' shared experiences, and the need for a response to financial marginalization. They kept spinning out ideas for financial integration and opportunity. Finally, they were ready to move. In 2018, four years after they met, they launched Esusu—a financial technology company meant to help low- to moderate-income renters use rent payments to build credit, establish a financial history, and make their way into the U.S. economy.

The name of the organization itself offered a look at their motivations and their plans to make change. The word *esusu* describes a traditional form of informal financing that originated in Nigeria, helping individuals and communities band together in savings and credit associations. The notion is that by working together in partnerships, people without a formal financial identity can help each other live and work in a mutually beneficial way.

That's the idea Abbey and Samir brought to the table when they participated in The Global Good Fund in 2019. The notion was a novel one, but it made sense; millions of people who are low-income in America make rental payments on time every month for decades without establishing a credit score. Meanwhile, landlords have no way of knowing which tenants are good bets. Esusu brought these communities together, partnering with landlords through a rent reporting service and helping low-income renters build credit by reporting monthly payments to credit bureaus. The organization even created a rent relief fund to help struggling tenants stay in their homes—a part of the company that quite literally saved lives during the worst days of the COVID-19 pandemic. Ultimately, the project was good for everyone: for renters, who could build credit; for landlords, who could ensure reliable tenants; and for the United States economy, which gained an influx of participants who could land jobs, pay taxes, and start their own businesses.

Getting Esusu off the ground wasn't easy. As Black and Brown business leaders, Abbey and Samir faced resistance from a venture capital community that overwhelmingly funds nondiverse entrepreneurs. They were forced to grapple with unfair assumptions about their competence and decision-making, and about the ability of a business focused on the racial wealth gap to survive. But with extraordinary drive and persistence, Abbey and Samir were able to forge their vision into a reality.

Today, Esusu is thriving, drawing investors from The Global Good Fund II to tennis superstar Serena Williams's Serena Ventures. The families that rely on its services are flourishing. Abbey and Samir continue pressing to expand their reach and uplift communities across the country, one rental payment at a time. According to Samir and Abbey, "Where you come from, the color of your skin, and your financial identity should never determine where you end up in life. Today there are over 45 million adults in America with no credit score, the vast majority of whom are immigrants, minorities, and low- to moderate-income households. The benefit of the Esusu platform is that everyone wins. It's a win for renters, property owners, and society at large."

In many ways, the story of Samir and Abbey is one of improbable success. It is a story of perseverance, hard work, and creativity; of connecting people and ideas in order to promote a cause that serves humanity.

It is the story of citizen statespeople.

The Road Ahead

It can feel difficult to make a difference. That's because it *is* difficult to make a difference.

The world faces enormous challenges and existential threats. An international health emergency impacts every country on the planet. Climate change causes extreme weather events that claim lives and livelihoods. Wars and violent conflicts spur refugee crises and population shifts. Economic inequality is growing, leaving millions of people in poverty in the shadow of a wealthy few. From proliferation of nuclear weapons to the hardening of political polarization and an increase in racial and social injustice, people in the United States and around the world face a dizzying array of complex and dangerous threats.

These concerns are deeply felt. According to a 2019 Pew Research survey,[1] most Americans expect income gaps to widen over the next three decades. Nearly half anticipate that the standard of living in the United States will get worse by 2050, while just 20 percent believe it will improve. Almost 60 percent say the condition of the environment will deteriorate. Nearly two-thirds of Americans expect political divisions to intensify, making it even more difficult to solve problems together.

Exacerbating these challenges is the fact that, in many cases, people have lost faith in the institutions charged with supporting and guiding us towards progress. According to a series of Gallup polls in 2021, just 38 percent of Americans have "a great deal" or "a lot of" confidence in the presidency. Big business scores lower, at just 18 percent. The media fares just as poorly; only 21 percent of Americans feel confident about newspapers, and 16 percent say the same of television news. Confidence in Congress, meanwhile, sits at just 12 percent.[2] Nearly every institution of note in the United States—from our lawmaking bodies to our executive powers to our economic engines and the arbiters of our public forums—is viewed with suspicion and doubt.

These low scores translate into real-world impacts. When people lose confidence in politics and political institutions, for example, they tend to gravitate towards behaviors and ideologies less likely to lead to cooperation and more likely to create dysfunctional systems. They might decide not to vote at all, producing an electorate unrepresentative of the community as a whole and a government that doesn't take their needs into account. They might drift towards extreme political views offering a scapegoat to blame or a place of refuge for disenchanted individuals. At the furthest end of the spectrum, they could lose faith in democracy as a whole and instead submit to authoritarian individuals or agendas. These results, in turn, breed further alienation and more dysfunctional politics.

The same kind of result is possible in other areas. A lack of confidence in the news media may prompt individuals to avoid learning about current events, or to dismiss facts, or to embrace fringe broadcasters with extreme viewpoints. Distrust of financial institutions or businesses could discourage individuals or communities from meaningfully participating in the economy, calcifying poverty, and walling off populations from economic growth. Over time, our cynicism can contribute to an age of inflamed tensions, widespread division, hypernationalism, and xenophobia—without trust in institutions, we are left with limited avenues for progress. We are regularly confronted by problems, but we don't believe our existing power structures will effectively step in to address them.

That's the bad news.

Here's the good news: even as we grapple with entrenched challenges and deteriorated institutions, we simultaneously live in an age of superpowered and super-engaged individuals. The Internet and mobile telephony have brought once-obscure information to our fingertips, enabling people to learn about problems and dig deep into tools for solutions. Technology lowered the barriers to entry for starting a company, supporting a cause, and spurring a social movement. Increased connectivity is making it easier for a person not only to take action in their own community, but to scale their efforts quickly and effectively—allowing good ideas to find larger audiences and create broader global impact.

The intersection of these dynamics is clear:

1. We live in a time where people have lost confidence in traditional institutions of power.
2. We live in an age of the superpowered individual committed to driving change in meaningful and multifaceted ways.

Increasingly, we struggle to engage institutions to tackle pressing challenges—but at the same time, individuals have the power like never before to step into the void. These circumstances create opportunities for the rise of citizen statespeople: individuals who are well equipped to take on and engage with the most complex issues society faces.

The Citizen Statesperson

The citizen statesperson is not just a superpowered individual; the citizen statesperson is a superpowered individual who is committed to improving one's community and the world. Not content to sit idly on the sidelines as a mere critic of events, the citizen statesperson is an active participant in the work of the moment, and the epitome of Teddy Roosevelt's "man in the arena" who labors in the pursuit of a worthy cause:

It is not the critic who counts, not the man who points out how the strong man stumbles, or where the doer of deeds could have done them better. The credit belongs to the man who is actually in the arena, whose face is marred by dust and sweat and blood; who strives valiantly; who errs, who comes short again and again, because there is no effort without error and shortcoming; but who does actually strive to do the deeds; who knows great devotions; who spends himself in a worthy cause; who at the best knows in the end the triumph of high achievement, and who at the worst, if he fails, at least fails while daring greatly, so that his place shall never be with those cold and timid souls who neither know victory nor defeat.

Of course, not every challenge comes with dust, sweat, and blood, and not every person in the arena will share the same characteristics, but there are certain qualities that tend to mark citizen statespeople and enable them to create an effective impact. We identify 10 of those key traits:

1. **Drive.** Citizen statespeople are driven, both by philosophical integrity and by the desire for practical experience, to understand other perspectives firsthand. Citizen statespeople share a deep commitment to an internal moral compass; they are equally dedicated to truly understanding peoples' perspectives and struggles in order to advocate on behalf of others. A citizen statesperson wants to change the status quo, and the inertia behind it. If you want to have a positive impact, you need to generate enough kinetic force to push against institutional forces. That requires relentless drive.

2. **Practicality.** Citizen statespeople believe in progress, optimism, and catalyzing the change they seek. They are doers who want to effect real change in tangible ways that impact peoples' everyday lives. That means being grounded in what is possible as well as understanding the levers required to make an impact. Citizen statespeople are not ivory tower philosophers cut off from the real world around them. Instead, they are connectors and achievers who view progress as the next logical stage of development—and are committed to take the actions necessary to achieve that progress.

3. **Perspective.** Citizen statespeople possess a sense of scale, recognizing global contexts and local impact alike. They are capable of seeing the interconnectivity of the world around them; understanding that the universe is bigger than they are, while also recognizing that they possess the capacity to catalyze important change. A citizen statesperson understands that they cannot make change at scale all by themselves— and also recognizes their potential as a catalyst and an agent of progress.

4. **Realism.** Citizen statespeople are realistic about where power and influence reside, and clear-eyed about the difficulty of

creating meaningful and enduring change. By homing in on critical details and recognizing the way people, communities, institutions, and power structures operate, citizen statespeople help identify tangible steps along the road to progress. Realism helps differentiate idealists from citizen statespeople; by closely observing the world around them, citizen statespeople weave components, ideas, and communities in new and impactful ways.

5. **Focus.** A citizen statesperson's most valuable resources are their time and energy—both are limited. As a result, citizen statespeople focus on their objectives and commit wholeheartedly to their goals in order to "move the ball forward." That doesn't mean citizen statespeople are incapable of doing multiple things at once; it does mean that they are capable of persevering through distractions and disruptions.

6. **Leadership.** Very few large-scale issues can be solved or addressed by one person working in isolation. Instead, a citizen statesperson builds a coalition of like-minded people to create change together. That process involves persuading, encouraging, and galvanizing others to comprise part of a larger solution. By exercising their own leadership, citizen statespeople advance and evolve society at large.

7. **Scale.** Making change in a person's local neighborhood or community is a great way to learn the basics of citizen statespersonship. Beyond that local focus, a citizen statesperson is also committed to taking their individual or group message to a larger audience to find how they can positively impact a greater number of people across borders or across stakeholder groups. That effort requires not only an understanding of how to broaden messages and scale change, but also a desire to shift from intimate local impact to extensive, far-reaching transformations. It is not an easy journey and it is often uncomfortable—commitment to pursuing progress at scale is at the heart of citizen statespersonship.

8. **Prioritization.** Here's a hard truth: you can't do everything at once, and you can't help everyone at all times. We're all pulled and tugged in a variety of directions. Many causes and needs concurrently compete for our limited attention. A citizen statesperson recognizes that, if we are always chasing the squeakiest wheel, we'll never be able to move in the most efficient or effective way. Instead, a citizen statesperson envisions a path towards progress, and then takes deliberate actions that are necessary to reach their goals. There may be times when priorities must be reassessed or reordered as a result of changing circumstances, and a citizen statesperson shouldn't be so committed to an initial planned route as to be incapable of flexibility—even in the most challenging of times, citizen statespeople can course-correct to plot and navigate a clear path forward.

9. **Openness.** Citizen statespeople believe that by engaging with problems and collaborating with others, they can find or create constructive solutions. In order to do that, they need to be open to new opportunities, new relationships, new communities, and new ideas—capable of interacting with people, places, and stories outside of their own lived experiences. That's why citizen statespeople are willing to leave their comfort zones, walk in multiple worlds and contexts, and parlay their understanding of real-life conditions to make a difference.

10. **Values.** Values are at the core of everything a citizen statesperson does. They guide our behavior when no one is watching, and drive our commitment to progress. Values help determine how we want to achieve our goals, and help decide what kind of leader we want to be. Values create clarity of purpose, and keep us focused on the priorities that matter. Citizen statespeople position values at the center of the work that they do. Developing clear understanding of those values enables citizen statespeople to set a course that aligns with their views, ethics, and ideals.

These ten traits are not exhaustive, and do not constitute a magic elixir for creating progress out of thin air; rather, they are qualities that help an individual become an effective citizen statesperson. These traits help guide a citizen statesperson through risks, challenges, and hard decisions. They empower a citizen statesperson to build a network, to broaden their views, and to drive impact at a global level.

In short, people who have these traits have the power to change the world.

Becoming a Citizen Statesperson

What do you need to become a citizen statesperson?

Let's start with what you *don't* need. You don't need extraordinary wealth or resources. You don't need important social or political connections. You don't need an army of enthusiastic supporters dedicated to achieving your success.

What you do need is a commitment to create positive change, and the will to see it through.

Consider Reyhan Jamalova's story. In her small village of Baku, Azerbaijan, the schools didn't teach science, technology, engineering, and math. Girls were largely expected to be married by age 17 and to devote their lives to their families. But Reyhan was drawn to science—and when she received the highest score on the entrance exam to a competitive school in Buka at 12 years old, she left her family to study and pursue a better education.

Reyhan quickly discovered that she was interested not only in learning, but in action. In Azerbaijan, strong rains frequently cause temporary electrical outages. Reyhan wondered whether one challenge could be used to solve the other, and whether rainwater could be used to generate energy. For four months, she and a friend, assisted by mentors, ran calculations and developed a device capable of doing exactly that. With financial support from the Azerbaijani government, Reyhan built her first prototype.

Her goal was to present her product at the 2017 Climate-Launchpad, the world's biggest green business competition. But in an accident, the generator shut down four days before the national final. In desperation, the team turned to two of the country's leading engineers, who told them that rebuilding the prototype in the time remaining was impossible. Undeterred, Reyhan and her team worked nonstop to re-create their model—and won the "Audience Favorite Startup" award in the ClimateLaunchpad competition.

She was just 15 years old.

Since then, Reyhan secured new investors and considered broadening her work to additional countries like the Philippines, India, Malaysia, and Indonesia, where monsoons are frequent, taking her idea and her entrepreneurial drive to new heights.

Reyhan didn't start her journey with immense stores of resources or broad support networks. Rather, she tapped into her driving passion to make an impact, and determined to push through challenges to reach her goals.

We know that individuals play critical roles in starting movements, for good or for ill. We've seen these movements play out in the last few decades. A merchant sets himself on fire and ignites the Arab Spring. A schoolgirl from Pakistan survives an assassin's bullet and fights for the right for women in her society to access education. A young Swedish activist challenges world leaders to address climate change, spurring global protests by millions of young people demanding a better future.

Of course, not every individual-led movement succeeds or crystalizes into positive impact. That's why there's more to being a citizen statesperson than being the symbol of a campaign or a liaison to global powers. To be a citizen statesperson, you must shape the dialogue and outcome according to your values. You must build social currency over time through social change efforts. And you must strive to play a meaningful and constructive role in helping to solve big problems in areas where traditional institutions have fallen short.

At their best, a political statesperson and a citizen statesperson do the same things; they bring people together, they forge solutions through diplomacy, and they push for agendas and social changes that benefit society. The difference is that a political statesperson is someone who represents his or her country or community in an appointed role, while a citizen statesperson is self-appointed—spurred by civic responsibility to take on larger challenges and harness a force for good in the world.

That's why the values we're discussing are so critical. Without drive, a person can't find the motivation to get involved in civic work. Without practicality, one can't navigate existing obstacles. Without perspective, one can't envision the impact that is possible through their own applied effort. The values that describe citizen statespeople—from realism to focus to leadership to scale—don't just help citizen statespeople achieve their goals; they also get regular people to the starting gate, helping others achieve their potential and become citizen statespeople themselves.

From Local to Global

Evolving into a citizen statesperson often starts at a local level, solving problems for local people. In some cases, this kind of service can manifest a form of training; an opportunity to become educated as a leader while positioning yourself to make a unique and outsized impact. Local service also teaches you how to find the heart of a challenge—to get as close as possible to decision-makers and stakeholders to design solutions and make a difference. From there, you can build awareness about an issue by engaging media or by protesting injustice. You can meet concerned individuals and put people and powerbrokers in the same room. If you can make an impact in your neighborhood, you can look outward to similar challenges that impact larger communities and affect broader populations; scale your service outward to apply your knowledge to more expansive issues.

This kind of outward progression isn't theoretical. It's real.

As a young person in Nigeria, Mene Blessing witnessed the challenges facing agricultural workers on the continent. With 80 percent of smallholder farmers in Africa subsisting on an income of less than $2 a day, meeting the high cost of food for poultry and livestock is often a challenge. His personal experience led him to set up Unorthodox Feeds Innovation for Rural Enterprising Smallholder Farmers, or UNFIRE—a program that provides farmers with feed costing 60 percent less than regular options, enabling farmers to increase their output and their incomes by as much as 80 percent. Produced from agricultural waste, such as mango seed kernels, elephant grass, maize, and cassava waste from milling plants, UNFIRE's feed is unique, culturally acceptable, and suitable for a range of poultry and livestock. It's sustainably produced, too, with UNFIRE operating a community-based, self-supportive model. Local youth groups are engaged in the collection of fair-trade raw materials that are purchased by UNFIRE, and rural women are recruited, trained, and empowered to run their own businesses as vendors, supplying and selling the feed within their own communities. The model was designed to benefit both farmers and their communities.

The program worked. During Mene's pilot, some 58 tons of mango seed waste was recovered and used by UNFIRE teams as part of a partnership with JA Farms in Nigeria. During an 18-month pilot program, 5,000 consumers benefited. Twenty-seven young people were engaged to help collect raw materials and 10 women vendors were employed to sell the seed. Each of these vendors, who were previously unemployed, generated the equivalent of local minimum wage. More than 14 million grams of livestock products were produced over the 18-month period, including 45,000 eggs and 3,070 chickens.

Mene didn't stop there. Instead, he built his work further, and went on to co-found and become COO of Vetsark, a data science social enterprise working to help predict and prevent disease and pest outbreaks in Nigeria. He used his success to help develop other citizen-statespeople; in 2016, he co-founded Inspire Africa—a Pan-African institution designed to transform the careers and life trajectories of a new generation of leaders and entrepreneurs in Africa by delivering high-impact entrepreneurship and leadership education to African youth. Against the backdrop of Nigeria's 58.1 percent youth unemployment rate, Inspire Africa trained 3,000 young people, helped fund more than 120 business ventures, and created more than 300 jobs.

Mene was not groomed into office by a political patron. He wasn't given a public platform by a well-heeled relative. Instead, Mene harnessed his ability to make an impact by using his values and skills to build a coalition for change. He appointed himself to solve hunger in Africa, helping to support farmers and consumers alike. Then he appointed himself to address the education to employment gap, enabling young peers to compete in today's evolving markets and ensuring that talent does not remain on the sideline. Mene's journey is just beginning; as a citizen-statesperson, Mene is still looking for ways to expand impact outward, to develop effective solutions, and to fuel ever-larger change.

That's how an individual can use local knowledge to make a global impact. For people around the world, that's how one citizen statesperson's leadership can change lives and set a new course for the future. That's the power of a citizen-statesperson.

Discussion Questions
- How do you embody the traits of a citizen statesperson?
- What values drive your interest in citizen statespersonship?
- What does your local community look like? What community is at the heart of the change you want to make?

Notes

1. John Gramlich, "Looking ahead to 2050, Americans are pessimistic about many aspects of life in U.S.," Pew Research Center, March 21, 2019, https://www.pewresearch.org/fact-tank/2019/03/21/looking-ahead-to-2050-americans-are-pessimistic-about-many-aspects-of-life-in-u-s/.
2. Megan Brenan, "Americans' Confidence in Major U.S. Institutions Dips," Gallup, July 14, 2021, https://news.gallup.com/poll/352316/americans-confidence-major-institutions-dips.aspx.

2

What It Takes

Key Takeaways

- A citizen statesperson finds opportunities to develop leadership skills, follow their passion, and make a difference in local communities and on a global level.
- Acting as a citizen statesperson puts demands on finances, time, and relationships. Passion and drive make the tradeoff worthwhile.
- A citizen statesperson is uniquely positioned to adopt a multifaceted viewpoint that helps develop unlikely solutions to advance a cause.

BEING A CITIZEN statesperson is issue- and geographically agnostic. That's not to say that citizen statespeople aren't passionate about specific issues or focused on specific places; to the contrary, a deep interest in an issue can be essential to progress, and a sense of place—a commitment to a local community or population—can help a citizen statesperson build social capital and create an effective movement. Instead, what it means is that passion around any issue offers the opportunity for citizen statespersonship, and any location or community can be a hub and launching pad for change. In that way, citizen statespersonship has the ability to cut through the greatest challenges of our time, providing a universal mentality and approach capable of solving problems at scale.

The ability to look beyond a specific place or a specific issue area is a useful asset. Today, the world is more interconnected and interdependent than ever before. As a result, most major challenges transcend geographic boundaries. At the same time, few problems can be placed into clear-cut subject or topical boxes; from economic hardship to climate change, from violent conflicts to social justice, individual challenges often have cross-cutting roots and expansive impacts. The ability to work across disciplines and issue areas proves immensely helpful.

That mentality—understanding the value of context and connections—is key, because being a citizen statesperson requires the skill to connect meaningfully with others. The citizen statesperson thinks about how to convene people, how to gain knowledge through dialogue, and, ultimately, how to use the power of one-on-one interactions to move issues forward. Whether you are acting as a citizen statesperson locally or working abroad—and whether your work is narrowly focused or more expansive—openness to these connections allows you to have greater impact in your community and in the causes most important to you.

The Benefits of Becoming a Citizen Statesperson

Being a citizen statesperson comes with tangible benefits. It spurs leadership development, harnesses passion to drive impact, and can lead to extraordinary and fascinating careers that set the stage for global progress. In fact, the process of becoming a citizen statesperson—interacting with others, finding learning opportunities, and building social capital—provides incredible value, because it offers an up-close, high-resolution view of leaders of different stripes. In a way, interacting with a variety of leaders is the best way to learn leadership. It's like an apprenticeship program: it allows you to observe the traits and behaviors of other leaders to bring some of those qualities into your own toolkit.

Having to be a connector, a bridge, and a negotiator also requires a citizen statesperson to navigate complex situations and play a diplomatic role. That process can teach you to tap into your empathy, train you to envision better outcomes, and build your patience and resolve for creating systemic change. Those are not easy qualities to learn. These days, we often find ourselves confined to echo chambers of people who emphasize similar beliefs. In a world of sound bites and social media, we are frequently presented with simplified arguments and us-versus-them approaches that do more to inflame tensions than solve problems. The citizen statesperson experience is an antidote because it requires you to see other people's perspectives, consider nuances and new angles, and play an intermediary role to find collaborative solutions.

Citizen statespeople come to learn that leadership skills are developed, not innate, and it's only through doing—through watching leaders, interacting with leaders, and collaborating with leaders on challenging issues—that you truly enhance your own toolkit. Public speaking skills, moderating and facilitation skills, thinking through how ideas and people could benefit from one another or the cause, convening, conveying ideas clearly through the written word, and choosing causes that unite diverse people—these are all skills that a citizen statesperson comes to embrace.

Of course, taking on the role of a citizen statesperson doesn't only provide you with a chance to hone important skills; it also opens the door to incredible opportunities and experiences. Every time you open one door, another door opens. When you engage with opportunities for citizen statespersonship, you are likely to interact with other citizen statespeople—that experience can present you with fresh contacts and new chances to make an impact.

The Challenges of Being a Citizen Statesperson

Here's the truth: there are aspects of being a citizen statesperson you may not like. You may not like the time investment required to forge meaningful relationships, especially with people with whom you don't see eye-to-eye. You may not like the attention you garner for being a citizen statesperson, especially if you have an introverted personality or feel uncomfortable in social situations. You may not like the potential controversy being a citizen statesperson stirs up when you take a position out of principle.

These are trade-offs that we understand. In 2016, we were both offered the opportunity to participate in the Eisenhower Fellowship—a program designed to connect and inspire leaders around the world and create a global network of change agents who are committed to a society that is more peaceful, more prosperous, and more just. It was an opportunity to travel abroad to other communities, to see change in context, and to join with other people passionate about making a positive difference.

Sounds great, right?

It also meant spending a full month away from home and family. At the time, we each had young children. We each had partners who needed to shoulder a greater share of responsibilities on the home front in our prolonged absence. We each had ongoing professional responsibilities and social networks that we would need to leave behind.

We also had individual considerations. Carrie had a one-year-old child and was helming a three-year-old organization. She had been on her version of maternity leave the year before, and was now considering the prospect of absence for a month, with no ability to check in regularly with the remaining leadership team. Two weeks before Carrie was supposed to depart for China, the person tasked with helping care for her child pulled out, leaving Carrie and her husband scrambling for additional support.

Yet even with these challenges, Carrie was committed to the project, because to Carrie, the opportunity costs of the fellowship outweighed its benefits. The fellowship offered the chance to see the world differently, to learn about a different culture, and to understand policy and business in a completely new context. The fellowship also presented Carrie with new contacts and connections; as one of the younger people selected for the fellowship, she was able to learn from a wide variety of accomplished individuals.

In fact, in Carrie's thinking, even the costs themselves had benefits. After her hired help pulled out, she was in a privileged position to ask her parents to help—and so while she had to spend a month away from her family, in exchange, her parents were able to spend time with their grandson uninterrupted. While she was absent from her organization, she was able to give her support team—and especially her chief operating officer— the experience of leading an expansive and growing nonprofit. While she was out of contact with her supporters and allies, donors were able to connect with other people on her team in new ways. Her husband—who had been supportive of her decision from the beginning—engaged in new ways on the home front in her absence.

Dean was likewise facing his own constellation of challenges. He had a three-year-old child at home with his wife, and so he required the same kind of family support. He had a very busy day job as a partner at a global law firm, which meant a huge transition for him and for his legal practice. There were financial considerations for a month-long absence. And yet, in conversations with his wife, it was always clear that the question was how to take advantage of this opportunity, not whether to pursue it.

In Dean's view, the interaction between the United States and China was shaping up to be the most critical geopolitical relationship on the planet. The Eisenhower Fellowship offered the chance to be at the center of it all, and to take a step back from legal transactions in order to focus on a broader understanding of how the world worked. For Dean, it was a long-term consideration: 20 years later, were his kids going to be prouder if he experienced this fellowship, or if he had a few more dollars in his pocket? What experience would define him and evolve his thinking about the world around him? While he had done a fair amount of legal work in China, the ability to spend a month meeting with leaders from across government and throughout the nonprofit and business sectors presented a chance for personal and professional enrichment that would otherwise have been impossible.

At the end of the day, for both of us, the decision primarily came down to three considerations. First, the opportunity offered long-term benefits that outweighed the short-term sacrifices. Second, the decision felt positive in the moment; that is, while we understood the drawbacks, it still made us feel excited to engage in an experience that would expand our horizons. Third, the decision to participate was supported by our convictions, and our belief in citizen statespersonship as an engine of progress.

Some people might have a difficult time understanding why any parent would choose to leave an infant child at home for a month in order to traverse the planet, meet other people, engage in conversations, and learn—and the truth is, it wasn't easy. But we both believed that being a citizen statesperson was the most meaningful way to create systemic, long-term positive change. We believed that it was important to our children's long-term future, and the future of their global community, for us to be able to make the greatest possible positive impact on the world around them. And we were committed to fulfilling our own roles as changemakers—not only when it was easy, but especially when it was hard.

Of course, being a citizen statesperson doesn't only mean investing your time. It also means understanding the value of financial investments in your professional development. That shouldn't involve harming your financial security or putting yourself in dire straits, but it may require making reasonable, consistent investments in your own training and opportunities to grow as a citizen statesperson. Over time, for example, if you are able to put aside $100 per month, you can save $1,200 every year—meaning that every other year, you can go to a major conference that makes a dramatic difference in who you are able to meet and the platforms you can experience. Think of it as a venture capital (VC) fund for your personal development.

Like any VC fund, your investment of time and money can spur others to invest as well. True story: at age 22, Carrie wondered aloud to her mentor, Larry Warren, who was then the CEO of Howard University Hospital, why more health systems didn't engage young people to serve on their boards. Three years later, Carrie participated in a women's governance training program to help women prepare for board placement. The program was expensive, so Carrie put as much of her own money toward the program as she could before asking for help by fundraising the rest of the fees. By showing that she was eager to dedicate her time and money for the training, others (shout out to C.E. Andrews) became willing to invest in her too. The lesson was that she shouldn't expect anyone to invest in her if she didn't invest in herself first.

But it wasn't just her financial investment that paid dividends. Carrie also spent a great deal of time emailing and arranging conversations with many people she aspired to learn from. Quite a few responded to her emails and were willing to answer her questions, which helped Carrie prepare for life as a citizen statesperson by uncovering important insights early. Twelve years later, one of the people Carrie asked her questions to—her old mentor, Larry Warren—reached out to ask if Carrie would be interested in serving on a health system board.

Carrie hadn't just idly wondered about the viability of youth participation on health system boards; she had spent years working on the issue, positioning herself to be a sought-out resource in helping to diversify boards and routinely introducing board candidates through The Global Good Fund network—the organization Carrie leads. That investment of time and energy paid off—and presented her with an opportunity to serve on the Trinity Health board, a $20 billion organization where Carrie serves today.

That story points to another important lesson: it's important to make known what you want to learn and achieve. Your networks will crystalize opportunities once they know your interests. In fact, that's how this book came to be in the first place: being vocal about our interests is what led us to learn about the Eisenhower fellowship, how we discovered a remarkable opportunity to participate—and how we met each other and began writing this book together three years later.

Time is a finite resource, so there will always be trade-offs and costs to taking action. If you feel a sense of conviction and you're excited about the opportunity, don't let naysayers or obstacles stop you from achieving your goals.

A Unique Value Proposition

Let's take a moment to understand what sets citizen statespeople apart from other individuals interested in change. We don't see ourselves as protesters. We're not angry fanatics. Citizen statespeople stand in contrast to more strident voices and forces like populism and radicalism because we don't just want to protest an unjust or unacceptable status quo; we want to find and achieve an effective solution. That's not to say that protesters can't become citizen statespeople. Sometimes warriors become diplomats, and nonviolent protest movements play an important role in raising society's awareness of important issues, priming the larger community for change. But to find a solution—when society is ready to change—it's time for a citizen statesperson to step into the breach.

Being a citizen statesperson means you are willing to engage outside of your own bubble by going to communities where you are uncomfortable, by meeting people where they are, and by engaging with views that might run completely counter to your own perspectives. In that sense, being a citizen statesperson is perhaps an antidote to the echo-chambers and self-segregation that we see in our public and private lives. Effective politicians often need to work across the aisle to move legislation over the finish line. In public leadership and social entrepreneurship alike, the way to drive impact is by bringing together stakeholders that are, to some degree, at odds with one another. Being a citizen statesperson, like all good diplomacy, is about understanding other peoples' perspectives, needs, and the pressures they face. This bridge-building capability is what gives a citizen statesperson the power to make a greater impact than a typical protester, activist, or government representative. It's the ability to bring people together around a set of common values and shared objectives.

You may think to yourself: What if I don't have that kind of insight? What if I don't have that kind of empathy? What if I don't always see the broader implications of policies and ideas, and how they affect others?

Here's the thing: few people are actually born with all these skills, and an instinct for empathy alone doesn't translate into effective citizen statespersonship. Instead, these are muscles one can develop and exercise, and attributes one can hone over time. By attuning oneself to a variety of roles and ways of thinking, one can learn to see the connections between people, proposals, and policy implications, develop the empathy needed to engage effectively, and learn the context that provides a useful background for effective solutions.

In other words, become a generalist.

It's rare for any major issue to be purely economic, purely legal, purely environmental, or purely social. Sometimes you want to hear what an entrepreneur has to say about a problem, because fast change and business engagement is key. Sometimes you'll want to connect with a policymaker, because the scope or scale of the problem is too broad for one sector to solve on its own. Sometimes you'll want to use a nonprofit approach because it's less tethered to certain societal pressures or bureaucratic constraints.

A citizen statesperson is the person who pulls together the threads, people, and resources to solve pressing challenges.

Anne Rweyora is an example of someone who has done exactly that. Anne grew up in Uganda, where nearly 70 percent of people live in substandard housing. That lack of quality housing compromises people's ability to achieve financial stability, provide for their children, and build community. After Anne's father passed away, she was homeless for 20 years—her experience drove her to find ways to support people in need.

As co-founder and CEO of Smart Havens Africa since 2018, Anne is directing her expertise into a mission to end housing poverty for vulnerable Ugandan communities. Her organization helps women and families acquire homes affordably through a rent-to-own model, moving homeowners towards legal ownership of the land where their house is built without the risk of being evicted.

Part of what makes Anne's operation so impressive is that she's addressing multiple objectives through one model. Smart Havens Africa's homes are environmentally friendly, using locally made interlocking blocks that don't need firing to meet climate goals set by the United Nations. At the same time, the homes are outfitted to use renewable energy and incorporate green innovations like rainwater harvesting systems and biodigestors that can turn waste into fertilizer.

Anne's organization also offers direct economic benefits. It provides training and apprenticeship for women and youth interested in careers in construction or real estate, and supports a local market where women, masons, apprentices, businesses, and clients can operate. According to Anne, building one home creates 13 direct jobs—and so far, Smart Havens Africa has constructed 80 homes for women and low-income families.

Finally, Smart Homes Africa promotes added social benefits by being thoughtful about where they construct houses and what resources are available to people nearby. By building homes in areas where most homes are owned by wealthy landowners, the company ensures residents will have access to good roads, power, water, health centers, and educational opportunities.

Anne didn't just find a novel way to increase quality housing in Uganda; she found a way to increase quality housing while also protecting the environment, creating jobs, and ensuring access to important services to generate multidimensional impact.

Cultivating a multifaceted viewpoint is something that you can do within your organization, within your interest area, and across industries. Just because a challenge doesn't fall within your experiential or academic expertise doesn't mean you can't make a difference; instead, use your diverse network with diverse perspectives to draw on the right support and expertise.

Dean has an instructive story here.

California boasts the fifth largest economy in the world, occupying a space between Germany and the United Kingdom. In areas from technology to the film industry, California's activity and leadership set the tone for other countries. And yet, historically, there has been no statewide governmental office in California dedicated to international policy—no secretary of foreign affairs, or minister of global action. To Dean, this felt like an oversight, a missed opportunity for collective problem-solving.

So he decided that citizen statespeople like himself should help take up the mantle of this role.

Of course, it wasn't that simple. He had to connect with the right people, engage in the right subject matter, and educate himself about the issues that mattered. But ultimately, he was able to take responsibility on himself and act on foreign policy not because he was an expert in the field, but because, as a citizen-statesperson, he was well suited to do the work. In the course of his efforts, he was made an honorary citizen of the German economy—a recognition of his tireless efforts to promote a stronger transatlantic relationship between Germany and California. He was able to organize events with the NATO secretary general to discuss the role of the alliance and the importance of innovation and California's tech sector in defending democratic values. He represented the state of California in trade and investment missions around the world. And he was able to host dialogues and conferences to connect government leaders from Asia, Europe, and South America with private-sector actors in Silicon Valley to build accessible conversations around issues that impact businesses and communities around the world.

Did the experience fit perfectly within Dean's area of expertise? No. Did he start with all the right information, and come from the right sector? Nope. But after years of cross-cutting experience and after developing relationships with other problem-solvers across the globe, he was able to draw on allies, connect partners, and cultivate supporters to help drive effective change.

That's citizen statespersonship.

Dean's example shows how a dedicated citizen statesperson can create change by considering what's missing in a given equation and adjusting one's own actions to fit the moment. But sometimes, opportunities for citizen statespersonship can arrive in a flash of inspiration, even when you're not expecting it.

Annie Ryu grew up in Minnesota and was pre-med at Harvard University when she traveled to India for the first time at

20 years old. At the time, her goal was to implement a maternal and child healthcare program she had developed with her brother. But that trip changed her plans, and altered the trajectory of her life, in a very unexpected way.

While she was traveling in India, she tasted a jackfruit—a tropical tree fruit that Annie compared to an "Indian porcupine." It was the best thing she had ever eaten—like a combination of mango, pineapple, and banana—but also nutritionally dense, high in fiber, low in calories, and with a meaty texture that can take on many flavors. It is also soy, gluten, nut, and cholesterol free, making it an excellent food source for health-conscious individuals or people with allergies. Annie learned that, although jackfruit is abundant in India, there is no international supply chain, and so most of the huge, green fruit grown in trees goes to waste.

The experience made a transformative impact on Annie's focus. Upon returning to school, she researched the U.S. market for plant-based food, met food experts, and traveled to meet with farmers in India. She saw an opportunity to transform thousands of farmers' lives for the better. And she developed a plan to help farmers in India while developing a market for jackfruit in the United States.

Today, as the founder and CEO of the Jackfruit Company in Boulder, Colorado, Annie is one of the most successful new entrepreneurs in the consumer food business. The company creates easy-to-prepare vegetarian dishes and features jackfruit as the primary ingredient. It works with more than 1,000 farming families in India that supply jackfruit to more than 6,000 retailers in the United States, and has become the largest jackfruit buyer in the world.

Annie didn't go to India expecting to join the food business. She certainly didn't anticipate that she would make a career out of agriculture in India, or that her work would support and sustain the livelihood of farmers in South Asia. But Annie did recognize an opportunity for citizen statespersonship when she saw it, and used that inspiration to change the world.

Making Connections in Unfamiliar Places

It's one thing to recognize the importance of connecting with disparate cultures and ideologies—it's another thing entirely to achieve it. Whether you are engaging with marginalized populations for a service project or connecting with affluent groups to discuss fundraising for an important issue, you will need to find ways to create comfort and connections with people different from you. Luckily, there are steps you can take, and principles you can bear in mind, to achieve exactly that.

First, begin by learning about the norms of the community. Much of this research can begin online, by reading about cultures and understanding the customs you might encounter. Consider looking at pictures to gain a visual sense of what you might see and experience. It's also important to explore human resources where available. Who do you know from the community who would give you a sense of what to expect? Who could you speak with to answer your questions, or give you suggestions for how to present yourself? If you don't ask, you don't know—and knowing can pay real dividends. When Carrie was spending time in places as disparate as China, India, and Nigeria, she did her homework online beforehand; she also asked individuals from each place how to show respect in the cultures she would be visiting. In China, she used two hands to receive business cards. In India, she bowed to people who were older than she was and used local names in the local language. In Nigeria, she was prepared for local customs around eating and drinking. Because she had spent time learning about these customs, she wasn't surprised by them, and they became a point of connection rather than division—allowing her to focus on more substantive matters.

Second, present yourself with care and thoughtfulness. Even the most assiduous research will leave holes in your knowledge. You will likely encounter situations that you weren't expecting—whether it's a living situation or a dietary practice or part of a foreign routine that is standard in the culture you're experiencing but feels new and different to you. The key is not to react with surprise or discomfort, but to maintain an openness and regard for traditions that are not your own. That might seem obvious, but it's also easier said than done, and different situations will provoke stronger reactions. Sleeping in a large room with lots of other people? That's a pretty easy adjustment. Eating a large live bug? That might be more challenging. As a citizen statesperson, you will often find yourself in territory that belongs to other people. Just as you would normally be respectful in another person's home, be deferential, considerate, and courteous when traveling to another person's country or community. That doesn't mean you can't have questions, but it does mean you ask questions in ways that are diplomatic, rather than probing. Framing a question as, "I know some people think X—do you agree, or do you have another view?" is a useful way to gain information without antagonizing others.

Third, citizen statespeople looking to connect in unfamiliar environments need to have self-discipline—and a thick skin. The unfortunate reality is that even your most valiant efforts to fit in might not ingratiate you to the community. Dean, for example, spent five years in East Asia, and a lot of time in Korea—but even after learning local customs and working to follow local practices, he was still sometimes singled out as a foreigner and a minority. That sometimes made him an object of ridicule or discrimination for people who didn't see complexity and simply ascribed to him their own caricatures of people from his background. At times, naturally, that could be frustrating. But at the end of the day, he concluded that while he couldn't control other people's actions, he could control his response by remaining respectful and staying focused on his larger goals—an attitude that helped make him successful.

The bottom line is this: if you want to be comfortable, make others comfortable. If you are conscientious, thoughtful in your presentation, and disciplined in your reactions, you will put your best foot forward and maximize your ability to connect, engage, and drive impact.

Discussion Questions

- What specific challenges are you facing as you seek to become a citizen statesperson? How will you navigate those challenges to connect, engage, and drive impact?
- What benefits do you see in citizen statespersonship?
- What new or unfamiliar cultures must you navigate to be effective? What steps will you take to work successfully within unfamiliar cultures ?

3

Life Cycle of a Citizen Statesperson

Key Takeaways

- The first phase of becoming a citizen statesperson involves finding your cause, building your personal brand, developing your knowledge base, and cultivating your network.
- The second phase of becoming a citizen statesperson involves leveraging your expertise and network to step into your leadership and become a catalyst for change.
- The third phase of becoming a citizen statesperson involves mentoring and developing emerging leaders to support your cause, thereby increasing your bandwidth for strategic involvement.

LOOK, WE GET it: the prospect of becoming a citizen statesperson sounds daunting. The journey involves learning about important causes, creating and maintaining a network, and investing in your professional development, all while searching for unique solutions to the world's most intractable challenges. That's a tall order.

So let's break it down. Citizen statespersonship isn't a static achievement; it's an ongoing effort to impact the world in varied, meaningful ways. That's why contemplating the life cycle of a citizen statesperson can be instructive. Consider designing yourself a framework to build a career that includes varied, meaningful actions at different points in your professional progression. You might start as an aspiring changemaker, transition to serve in an established role as an effective problem-solver, and perhaps one day use your experience to develop the next generation of leaders. Each citizen statesperson's journey is their own. What will your citizen statesperson journey look like? The life cycle of a citizen statesperson serves as a series of signposts to help you find your way forward and makes the journey less daunting at the outset.

Beginning Your Journey

Let's begin at the beginning. You're interested in making a difference, you possess the temperament for citizen states-personship, and you are motivated to drive change. But you're also new to the idea, and you're not sure how to get going. Maybe you're just starting out in your career. Maybe you don't have an expansive network. Maybe you've never organized a convening. Maybe you don't know the Secretary General of NATO (yet). Maybe you are partway through your career and are looking to pivot, but aren't sure how.

Don't panic! Everyone starts somewhere—by taking deliberate steps, you will find your footing and make important progress as a citizen statesperson.

Identify Your Cause

There are so many important issues that impact the daily lives and futures of people around the world. Trying to tackle these problems all at once would be overwhelming. Instead, begin by asking yourself open-ended questions to narrow your initial focus and identify your area of interest—for example: What causes matter to me? What are my passions? What changes do I want to see in the world? What are my areas of expertise? There are no wrong answers to these questions. What's important is that you take time to reflect deeply about what matters to you. Your responses will help shape your path forward.

Sometimes causes that matter to you will emerge from personal experiences. Justin Constantine, for example, was a military reservist in Iraq in 2006. While he was on patrol, he heard sniper fire, and moved to warn a reporter who had been traveling with him. In the next instant, Justin was struck with a bullet that penetrated his ear and exited through his mouth.

Justin went through an emergency tracheotomy, months in intensive care, two dozen operations, and a lengthy rehabilitation. Even today, Justin can't see out of his left eye; he's missing most of his teeth and the end of his tongue; he can't run because doctors removed bones from his legs to use in reconstructing his upper and lower jaws. He suffered from post-traumatic stress disorder (PTSD) as a result of his experience, and he has battled shame that comes from looking and sounding different than he did before his injury.

Justin would be the first to say that he's lucky to be alive. But for him, simply surviving was not enough. He wanted to draw on his experience and skills as a leader to change the lives of others. He was committed to helping veterans fight the stigma of mental health issues and disabilities and forge new career paths.

After he retired in 2013 as a lieutenant colonel, Justin co-founded the Veteran Success Resource Center—an organization that helps veterans transitioning out of the military. The group arranges events for veterans and their spouses or partners so they can help each other to find mental health services, jobs, and education. The organization hosts military markets for families to gather food, clothes, diapers, and other necessities for free. Most importantly, the Veteran Success Resource Center provides a community for people who want to connect with others who recognize and appreciate their stories.

Justin's story is unique. Not everyone is able to trace their chosen cause to a dramatic personal experience. A citizen statesperson might be inspired by online research, by a moving news story or documentary, by the experience of a loved one, or by a combination of one's own interests and values.

Veronika Scott's pioneering work came about because of a school assignment. As a student at the College for Creative Studies in Detroit, Michigan, Veronika was required to create a product that would meet a need in the community. She hit upon an answer that changed the course of her life—and the lives of people around the world.

During the cold Detroit winters, Veronika would often witness people without homes congregating around warming stations. As a person whose parents had experienced poverty and addiction, Veronika was interested in serving populations who experience homelessness. She decided to create a warm, durable, water-resistant coat that converted into a sleeping bag at night and could be rolled up and worn as a shoulder bag when not in use. Thus, the EMPWR coat was born.

What made Veronika's work special is that she didn't stop there. Even after she finished her school project, Veronika continued to design additional prototypes for the coat. She kept reiterating on better ways to serve the homeless population. She was motivated to help marginalized people around the world stay safe and protected.

One day, a woman experiencing homelessness told Veronika that while the coat provided warmth and shelter from the rain, it didn't provide the most crucial asset she needed: a job.

That interaction was the inspiration Veronika needed. She developed Empowerment Plan—an organization focused on providing full-time employment and supportive services to single parents experiencing homelessness in Detroit. Individuals employed by Empowerment Plan manufacture EMPWR coats, helping to keep others safe and warm. As part of Empowerment Plan's effort, 60 percent of an employee's day is spent in coat manufacturing while the remaining 40 percent is dedicated to programming and supportive services. In partnership with other organizations, Veronika's company offers professional development, GED courses, mental health assistance, domestic abuse support, and other critical services.

Empowerment Plan has been an extraordinary success. So far, all of the people hired by the company have moved into permanent housing within six weeks of starting work. The company says not one employee has become homeless again. And the EMPWR coat is distributed in all 50 states, 11 provinces and territories, and 20 countries around the world. There are retail versions of the coat for sale, purchased by people who want a warm, fashionable coat that supports a great cause.

Veronika's example demonstrates how a person can look at the world around them, identify a critical need, and get to work on a solution. It shows, too, that someone's first idea will likely not be the last. Continue to think deeply, iterate, and look for new ways to expand your reach and deepen your impact.

Your decisions matter, so take time to reflect. You don't need to make decisions alone. No one is forcing you to go out today and make a snap decision about what subject will guide your actions. Instead, read about pressing issues, talk to people you trust, and consider the topics that interest you, excite you, and resonate with your background.

Do you want to work on challenges surrounding gender equity and racial inclusion? Are you enthusiastic about combatting climate change or fighting for criminal justice reform? Will you get involved in sustainable agriculture, or accessible healthcare, or universal education? Over time, you will build a better understanding of your arena—providing a foundation for citizen statespersonship, and helping you become an effective problem-solver.

Build Your Personal Brand

Regardless of where you are in your journey of becoming a citizen statesperson, it's worthwhile to think about establishing and/or strengthening a professional brand that reflects your personal values, the issues you're focused on, and the resources, talent, and potential that you bring to any given situation.

There are a great many resources available with instructions about how to build a personal brand. What's different about building a brand as a citizen statesperson from building a traditional professional or personal brand?

The primary difference is that a citizen statesperson's brand is not limited to who you are; it's also about what you are trying to accomplish and why. You might have a personal brand that positions you as the best private wealth manager in your community, for example, but that doesn't make you a citizen statesperson. The question is, how are you using your brand to create a better world? Your brand is outwardly focused and aspirational—explaining not only your actions, but your motivations as well, and how you relate to others.

Being a citizen statesperson is about leadership. It's about an interest in public service, an ability to connect disparate people and ideas, and a desire to elevate public dialogue. The citizen statesperson seeks to put her personal imprint on issues that bring varied stakeholders together, solve complex problems, and ultimately improve the human condition. That's why your brand needs to reflect your cosmopolitan outlook and your mission-driven approach.

You might be surprised at how quickly you can cement a reputation as your community's resident expert on a topic you care about. These days, people tend to acquire a lot of second- and third-tier connections. Owing to online activity and social networks in particular, we add more people peripherally attached to our professional circles than ever before. Use those relationships to learn from others and to bolster your personal brand for impact. If you are effective in your branding as a citizen statesperson, you will quickly become known as an expert in your issue of choice. As you build your brand, it will become self-reinforcing—success will beget success in a virtuous cycle.

Ange Muyubira was born in Burundi—one of the poorest countries in the world, with more than 70 percent of its population living on less than $2 per day. She studied interpreting and translating in England. Although she was interested in language, she was passionate about art and fashion.

When Ange returned to Burundi after a decade in Europe, she created Burundi Tours and Events, which specialized in offering Burundian cultural tours to visitors. Foreign tourists often asked Ange if they could see how traditional Burundian art and crafts items were made. To her surprise, Ange found there was a lack of appealing, authentic Burundian souvenirs for purchase. Instead, most of the country's artisans were making old-fashioned craft objects that didn't sell well in the modern marketplace.

Ange sensed a niche in the market and a way to support vulnerable Burundians. She founded Kaz'O'zah Art—an ethical fashion organization that provides Burundian artisans with the skills, support, and market access they need to design, produce, and sell contemporary fashion and crafts. She created a four-month training program—the Art Innovation Incubator—to teach skills like weaving, jewelry making, woodworking, and leather craftsmanship, alongside training in business and entrepreneurship, information on how to form cooperatives, and health and sanitation guidelines. To help artisans market and sell their goods in world markets, her program also teaches English.

When the artisans complete the training program, they may be hired by Kaz'O'zah Art's for-profit arm or start their own cooperatives. Kaz'O'zah Art even helps artisans access lines of credit for emergencies. Ultimately, Ange's work is empowering Burundian artisans to become independent and self-sustaining while contributing to an economically and socially empowered East Africa.

Ange may have started out as an interpreter with an interest in fashion. But today, she is one of her community's foremost citizen statespeople, and a leader in ethical fashion and art.

Network with Others

Citizen statespeople are impressive, but they are not all-powerful. Instead, it's important to develop useful contacts, engage with connected organizations, and find partners in progress. That's why building a network is key.

Few people can solve big problems single-handedly, or make big changes through individual action.

"Networking" can feel like a loaded term, conjuring visions of smoky backrooms, seedy cocktail receptions, transactional horse-trading, and disingenuous backslapping. But the truth is that networking is simply about identifying and connecting with people who share your interests—and the process can start close to home.

Take inventory of the people in your network who already focus on the issues you care about. Consider family members, current and former colleagues, and social acquaintances. Review your existing email addresses, phone and social media contacts. You might find that you know more people than you think relevant to your cause as a citizen statesperson.

Ask your contacts to connect you with other people involved in the work you care about. If you want to focus on education reform, explore your social circles or social media networks to see if you know someone involved in similar efforts. Go on LinkedIn, search for the term "education reform," and see what you find. You may be surprised to discover how many experts on the topic are just one step removed from someone you know— and how open your primary connections are to making an introduction.

Organizations serving your issue area are excellent resources for expanding your network. You can identify groups focused on your topic through your own research, or you can work backwards by thinking about the individuals you would like to learn from, explore the organizations they are connected with, and request to join those organizations to receive the same newsfeeds and learn more about the subject matter(s) they cover. Participate in open events held by these organizations and introduce yourself to the key players. Connect with speakers who address the organization's forums, and with fellow attendees. You might be surprised to find unexpected collaborators.

Networking isn't a one-step process; it involves ongoing effort. So if you meet other individuals who share your interests, don't stop there. Learn their origin story about how they got involved in the issue you mutually care about. Dig online to find that information, or ask. Showing genuine interest in other people makes others more interested in sharing their personal journeys, particularly if you can connect with their lives outside of the present context of career development. You will likely learn important slivers of information about their upbringing that might resonate or give inspiration to your journey as a citizen statesperson. In the process, you can ask: What businesses, nonprofit organizations or individuals do they know that are involved in addressing the issue of import? Sometimes, networking is about being a detective and staying curious—the stronger your connections, the more effective you can be.

Networking need not always be formalized; it can also happen on an impromptu or *ad hoc* basis. If you hear about an issue that interests you on the news, take the time to learn more. What stakeholders are engaged in the policy process? Who are the decision-makers? How might you engage with the organizations or people who are working on this topic? If you don't know anyone at the organizations or offices you identify, reach out cold. You have nothing to lose. There is a mathematical limitation to what you can learn directly through your network. Your research is mission critical to connect you with new people.

Some years ago, Dean was poking around on the Internet when he came across an organization he had no idea existed, but it caught his attention because it operated in a space he was very interested in. He didn't personally know anyone involved, but he decided to reach out to the chair of the organization to have lunch—to discuss the organization and to learn about their work and how he might contribute. Over time, he found he knew people or got to know people. Dean got involved with the organization, and steadily worked his way up the chain, playing important roles in the leadership team. Today, he's the past chair of the organization—not because he waited for someone to tap him on the shoulder, but because he made it known in a professional manner that he cared, and was willing to go to great lengths to learn and contribute.

Networking is not a zero-sum game; lending some of your contacts on behalf of someone else doesn't mean that you have diminished or expended your network capital. In fact, the opposite is true: if you are successful at connecting someone with a great opportunity or new professional contact, you will create natural allies for your causes, expand your network and broaden your impact. So if you see great opportunities that are not for you, make a note of the opportunities, and consider whether they would be interesting to someone you know. Then connect the dots! If you come across an article on a topic that would interest a contact, send it along.

> *In finance, we talk about "arbitrage" as leveraging your information advantage against competitors. As a citizen statesperson, you need to do the opposite: use your knowledge to assist others and make information and opportunities available.*

Even in an age of social media and the Internet, when information can seem ubiquitous, distribution of information about opportunities is often asymmetrical. Not everyone will encounter or be aware of every opportunity.

Develop Your Knowledge

We get it: when you start out as a burgeoning citizen statesperson, it's easy to focus on the parts of the puzzle you may feel you *don't* possess. It's easy to feel stuck, and to fixate on the information or connections or skills you lack. If you feel that way, you're not alone. Few people start out on their mission of impact with all the answers.

Instead of wallowing in what you don't have, focus on what you *do* possess. Do you have a few connections? Assemble them for a symposium, and you'll have started building a reputation for yourself as a convener. Do you have access to insights or ideas on a topic that matters to you? Learn more and share what you know with others, and you'll be well on your way to cultivating your expertise. Do you know of some opportunities to get involved? Follow through on those opportunities, and soon you will have practical experience you can bring to bear.

Here's an example: the State Department operates a Global Ties and International Visitors Leadership Program (IVLP). These are exchange programs with decades of history that receive delegations from across the world. Even as a young professional with relatively spare life or work experience, you can identify a part of the world or a topic or issue you care about, find your local office of Global Ties, share your area of interest with them, and indicate that you are willing to gather leaders with shared interests to meet a delegation from another country. You effectively solve the chicken-and-the-egg problem; by providing what you do have—an interest and an audience—you can generate a partnership that provides the rest.

As you explore learning opportunities, don't let exorbitant prices or sticker shock discourage you. Instead, think about your VC fund for personal development. If you see an opportunity that particularly intrigues, write to the people in charge of the opportunity to share what you *can* contribute. Tell them *why* you are excited by the opportunity, what you will do as a result of the opportunity, and how it is important to you to "have skin in the game" by contributing financially what you can afford. You might be pleasantly surprised by your meaningful ability to participate in a learning opportunity you originally imagined would be off-limits.

In fact, spending money selectively and intentionally can help open doors. Even modest amounts of money, whatever that means to you, can move the needle and set you apart. It sends a signal that you are committed to the cause, and will encourage others to see you in a rarified light: as a person willing to expend their own precious resources in support of a worthy cause. Remember, the amount does not necessarily matter. We've witnessed citizen statespeople around the world contribute as little as $1 per month to a cause they care about. The point is that they are purposefully investing their own resources into the arena. Our advice is to spend the amount of money that makes you stay alert and keep your eye on the priority; that financial amount is different for each person. Staying true to your priorities along the journey to becoming a citizen statesperson will ultimately help you develop your knowledge in the priority areas that matter most to you.

It may not always be immediately clear how best to enter a field or arena. What is clear is that the number of opportunities you can expose yourself to and capitalize on increases exponentially when you are a curious and active seeker of those opportunities. Don't sit back and let opportunities come to you. Don't wait for a role to present itself through word-of-mouth. Your direct and secondary networks might be the most powerful, sharpest entry point into opportunities—but they aren't your only meaningful networks. Keep a list of potential opportunities, people, or organizations that interest you. Over time, follow through on the links that seem most exciting. Come back to them if they don't pan out, and keep searching for new chances to make a difference. For most of us, there's no good reason to delay getting started. We all have the potential to drive positive change. The more you seek to become an expert and seek to engage on an issue, the better equipped you become to do exactly that.

Sustaining Your Growth

Let's say you are no longer in the beginning stages of your career. Maybe you've been working for a decade or more. Maybe you have many great contacts, and you feel like you have the lay of the land. You've built a brand as a citizen statesperson, you've chosen topics that are important to you, and you've connected with organizations and attended events to deepen your knowledge.

What now?

This is an exciting time for a citizen statesperson because it offers the chance to capitalize on your expertise, network, and social standing to step into higher leadership and catalyze greater positive change.

Start again by thinking anew about your specific area of expertise and then expand or generalize that topic to consider the broader industry, sectors, and/or social influences that impact your industry and your world more broadly. Look from different standpoints at the organizations you belong to or have worked with and the roles you've held. For example, in different settings, a lawyer might align herself or speak in support of business owners, service providers, employers, or persons in need. The citizen statesperson is looking for opportunities to amplify her voice by finding common cause with other professionals in different areas of professional expertise who care about the same issues.

Another example: a financier, a lawyer, a marketing specialist or a clinician may be a citizen statesperson promoting climate change awareness, immigration rights, education reform, or trade and investment. These citizen statespeople deploy their professional platforms to address important policy and social issues. The educator or nurse who cares about climate change does not necessarily abandon her career to lead an environmental organization. Rather, that citizen statesperson might find a way to incorporate her unique voice and leverage her unique set of experiences.

There's precedent for this kind of work. In the 1990s, Gary Cohen—a committed environmentalist—learned about endocrine-disrupting chemicals like dioxins that were found in the environment, but tended to build up in the fatty tissues of humans and animals. Once they found their way in, these chemicals wreaked havoc on hormones, damaged the immune system, and even caused cancer. His expertise in environmentalism spurred his interest in the subject, but what he discovered next changed the course of his life. It turned out that one of the largest sources of dioxin emissions in the United States was hospitals.[1]

This revelation inspired Cohen to dig deeper. He took a closer look at hospitals' impact on the environment, and concluded that a range of hospital practices—from thermometer disposal to incinerator use—was damaging environmental health and public health alike. In response, he built an organization called Health Care Without Harm. Today, he is leading a global movement for environmentally responsible healthcare.

Cohen may not have intended at the outset to focus on the healthcare industry, nor did he abandon his environmental interests in order to pursue a new challenge. Instead, he applied his background and his expertise in an unexpected way, using his unique voice to answer a pressing and important challenge.

Of course, don't count on discovering your calling accidentally. Instead, actively search for new ways to learn and apply what you know. In order to do that, it's helpful to tackle projects that grow your skill set and expose you to new topics and ideas. Those new topics and ideas might not fall directly in your wheelhouse, but expanding your horizons will better enable you to think creatively and solve complicated problems effectively. Think of it this way: you may be strongest in tennis when you play to your forehand, but if you're constantly playing to your forehand, your playing range will stagnate, and then how much better can your game really get?

Career advisors tend to encourage people seeking to advance their career within a large organization to accept projects outside of their expertise that others may find less appealing. In the moment, this type of extra work may seem like a lateral career move. But later in a career, you'll bring something to problem-solving that colleagues may not because you developed your skill and expertise more broadly than your peers. The same philosophy applies to citizen statespersonship.

> *Broaden your stance to apply outside of your organization and outside of your industry. Acquire new skills that set you apart as a more successful problem-solver. Actively search for ways to learn and grow.*

Peter Thiel, the entrepreneur and venture capitalist, discusses a concept in his book *Zero to One* that is instructive here. He identifies two kinds of progress: horizontal progress and vertical progress. In effect, horizontal progress involves copying things that work, and traversing a path to success that has been blazed before. Horizontal progress, says Thiel, is easy to imagine, because we already know what it looks like.

Vertical progress, on the other hand, means doing new things, envisioning a fresh version of the future that others don't see, and developing a novel path to reach the intended future.

If you want to challenge yourself to grow, look for vertical opportunities—open your mind and remain receptive to learn something new. When you're a citizen statesperson, that hunger to grow doesn't stop, no matter where you are in your career.

Dedication to creative thinking is a cornerstone of citizen statespersonship. Let's imagine, for example, that the issue at hand is how to educate more women in the developing world, for purposes of advancing both human rights and economic conditions. If you're looking at this issue solely from a policy implementation perspective, you might take a top-down view about how to obtain funding or deploy resources.

But you are a citizen statesperson. First, you might talk to NGOs that understand what's happening on the ground, and can educate you on what's working and what's not working. Then you might connect with businesses that agree to fill vacant jobs with qualified women. Maybe you would partner with families, organizations, and communities that help women complete high school or technical training and obtain higher-paying jobs. Or maybe you'd look at myriad circumstances and perspectives and find a problem that needs to be solved upstream. As a citizen statesperson, you recognize that typically there's no silver-bullet answer, and that any solution will inevitably require pulling disparate groups together.

You don't have to be one of the major stakeholders to catalyze change. In fact, major stakeholders are often constrained by major blind spots.

Here's what we know:

Often the best catalysts are not the biggest players. The citizen statesperson tends to move more nimbly than larger stakeholders, and operates with fewer of the constraints that major stakeholders face—from the need for institutional buy-in to layers of time-consuming bureaucracy. Citizen statespeople also benefit from an outside, aerial view, coupled with an ability to mobilize people and resources. While big ideas might need to be brought into a larger ecosystem eventually in order to make expansive progress, initial concepts often derive from external inspiration.

In many cases, meaningful catalysis of change requires telling effective stories. In our view, the two most powerful forces elementally are ideas and persuasion. Ideas involve the vision to see the future, to perceive how circumstances can change, and to imagine what the new normal might be. That interest in imagining the future is core to progress. Persuasion, meanwhile, turns on the way we understand ourselves and our way in the world. As humans, we are hard-wired to understand ourselves through storytelling. It matters a lot less who is telling the story or how well worn that story is. What really matters is the power of the message, the values and inspiration behind it, and how well it resonates with who we are and who we aspire to be.

If you have an idea, and you can frame it in a compelling story, then you are a disruptor and a change agent, and there are very few established dogmas or structures that can stop you. You may sometimes be perceived as a small player—but you can wield a force-multiplier that can challenge the *status quo* and advance your values, ideals, and agenda to forge a better world. Entire companies and movements are built on this premise.

Take Esusu, the organization founded by Samir Goel and Abbey Wemimo. Esusu is designed to report rent payments to the three major credit bureaus to help renters build credit while also lowering evictions and filling apartment vacancies—maximizing property outcomes for managers and owners while empowering tenants to establish credit scores, lower interest rates, and overcome barriers to becoming homeowners. At the time of this book's writing, Esusu had reached more than 200,000 residents nationwide, 100 percent of Esusu's formerly credit-invisible participants now hold credit scores, and residents' average credit scores have improved by between 20 and 100 points.

Samir and Abbey didn't start out as obvious stakeholders or traditional powerbrokers, but their experiences informed the kind of impact they wanted to have. Samir's family arrived in the United States with no credit and were robbed when they arrived, leaving them with no access to money at all. When Abbey immigrated to the United States from Nigeria, he and his mother were turned away from banks because they lacked a financial history, and his mother was forced to pawn her wedding ring to help provide for her family. Through their work as citizen statespeople, Samir and Abbey became force multipliers— for 45 million Americans who are financially invisible and 150 million more who are financially unhealthy, Esusu serves as a bridge between the formal and the informal financial economy.

Amplifying Your Impact

A citizen statesperson's work is never done. But over time, you will become adept at leveraging your network for positive outcomes. It will be natural for you to hear about the types of opportunities that you have pursued throughout the course of your career. You will have cemented touch points—a kind of standard circuitry connecting the organizations and causes you care about.

This is the third stage of citizen statespersonship. Looking out for opportunities that enable you to keep advancing your causes is valuable—but during this stage, you can increase your impact by identifying other people to connect to those opportunities, by inspiring more individuals to take up the cause, and by helping to generate additional citizen statespeople to amplify your work outward.

When you are an earlier-career citizen statesperson, part of the value you bring to the table is your energy and your willingness to do anything—from providing content expertise to planning events to doing research and other critical legwork. As you advance further along in your career, your energies may be better spent at a more strategic or relationship level. If you're trying to evolve and find your highest and best use while also trying to function as the working level engine, you're likely stretching yourself thin. By bringing people along, you not only help other people grow while supporting the causes you care about, you also free your time and increase your bandwidth to apply your skills most effectively.

How do you make the most of this to amplify your impact as a citizen statesperson?

First, stay informed about available opportunities. Read the newsletters your organizations put out, check in with the network you have built, and ask questions about the work that is being done to make the world a better place. When those opportunities are not relevant to you—and even when they are—refer them to up-and-coming citizen statespeople.

Second, deploy your skills as a connector. Take the time to look at every opportunity that comes across your desk, whether it's a job or a fellowship or an event, with this question in mind: *Whom do I know who could benefit from this opportunity?* A citizen statesperson knows that there is power in identifying opportunities for other people, precisely because it is such a rare exercise. It's valuable to the person you present with a career-changing opportunity, it's a useful way to strengthen your own ties to an individual or to a cause, and it spurs an aspiring citizen-statesperson to grow their work and expand their own impact.

Third, subsidize an emerging citizen statesperson directly. Consider devoting some portion of your personal funds or resources to sponsor an emerging citizen statesperson to ensure that they can be involved in events or organizations that strengthen their work and train them to succeed. Just as your VC funds helped to invest in your career when you were starting out, you can also invest in other individuals in whom you see potential. Your subsidy could be a determining factor in making an opportunity possible for a rising star.

Developing mentees helps expose you to fresh ideas so that you continue to learn about the causes that matter to you; it's also a way to broaden your own impact. By investing in promising citizen-statespeople, you are a catalyst for their growth—and through continuing mentorship, you ensure that your ideas and social impact continue to live on.

Discussion Questions

- What cause—or causes—do you feel strongly about? Where do you think you might be able to make a difference through citizen statespersonship?
- What resources would be helpful in growing your expertise so that you can speak and act with authority on the issues you care about?
- What kind of network do you have in place that can help you grow your footprint in this area—and what steps do you need to take to develop your network further?

Note

1. Valerie M. Thomas and Thomas G. Spiro, An estimation of dioxin emissions in the United States. *Toxicological & Environmental Chemistry* 50 (1995), https://www.tandfonline.com/doi/abs/10.1080/02772249509358202.

4

A Citizen Statesperson's Environment

Key Takeaways

- Foundational pillars of democracy, political freedom, and human rights have faced setbacks in recent years, shaking faith in civic institutions and creating a more chaotic global landscape.
- Recent history has reshaped the role of the citizen statesperson, imposing new challenges and opportunities.
- Technology makes citizen statespersonship possible by allowing people to connect with others beyond their immediate circles, and by amplifying voices, presenting unprecedented opportunity to drive impact.

IN ORDER TO consider the role of the citizen statesperson today, it's helpful to think about how the world has evolved over the last century.

After the Second World War, the defeat of the Axis powers seemed to portend a more open, more democratic society. Adolf Hitler's Nazi ideology had been routed, Benito Mussolini's National Fascist Party had been dismantled, and Emperor Hirohito's Japan had been transformed into a constitutional monarchy that rested power with the people. Out of the wreckage of the League of Nations had grown a new organization—the United Nations—founded by 51 countries committed to maintaining international peace and security, developing friendly relations among nations and promoting social progress.

The aftermath of the Cold War nearly a half-century later reinforced that shift. The fall of the Berlin Wall, the disintegration of the Iron Curtain, and the collapse of the Soviet Union felt like a harbinger of a new, more connected, more open global market. Around the world, nations were throwing off the yoke of totalitarianism and oppression, giving a new voice to their people and offering new opportunities for action.

The postwar landscape appeared to confirm that the future belonged to those who could work together in the service of political and social liberalization, more active democratic participation, and freer economic interaction. First, democracy had triumphed over fascism; now, open markets had stymied communism as well. An expansive new global ecosystem was taking shape, with innovative and collaborative movements and organizations pointing the way toward peace, justice, and opportunity.

At that point, citizen statespeople might have considered it their role to help accelerate a rolling transformation, to add their energy to an effort that was already ongoing, and one that seemed poised for continued success.

Yet in recent years, that eagerly anticipated renaissance has struggled to advance, and in some cases has lost ground. According to Freedom House—an organization that conducts research and advocacy on democracy, political freedom, and human rights—2018 marked the 13th consecutive year in which global freedom declined, spanning countries in every region around the world.[1] Authoritarian governments have reasserted control in some nations, while even long-standing democracies—including the United States—have struggled with populist movements that have attacked core civil and political rights, from freedom of the press to separation of powers to protection of minority rights. Meanwhile, gaps between the rich and poor have widened, shaking faith in capitalism as a driver of shared prosperity.

Traditional alliances have also been frayed and upended. The United Nations has been riven by disagreements. The North Atlantic Treaty Organization (NATO), formed at the urging of the United States in the early days of the Cold War, came under fire from U.S. leaders during the Trump Administration. A world community that prized collaboration has fallen into disagreements, from skirmishes over how to deal with potential nuclear powers like Iran to quarrels over transatlantic partnerships for trade throughout Asia. At the outset of the COVID-19 pandemic, institutions that were designed to organize and manage coherent responses to international challenges largely fell by the wayside as individual countries tussled for scarce resources.

These shocks and trends have had a very real impact. The world's once-inevitable march towards a more free and collaborative future has stalled. The winds of change—which, for decades, appeared to blow calmly in the same general direction—have suddenly become much more unsettled.

What does this situation mean for a citizen statesperson?

In some cases, winds of change have contributed to the general distrust of institutions that has made citizen statespeople necessary. But the lack of a clear tailwind also means that citizen statespeople must make more difficult and complex choices about how to participate in the world. In such a chaotic climate, it's not enough simply to reinforce or accelerate the direction in which the world is already headed. Instead, citizen statespeople must decide what kind of world they want to live in, and then set a course for that future.

Is that a lot of pressure? Yes! Beyond charting a path forward toward a clear and obvious goal, citizen statespeople today must take a step back to look at the bigger picture to make strategic decisions about what kind of goal they intend to achieve. That exercise requires a fundamental sense of one's ideas about morality, progress, and vision of the world. What is right and wrong? What does a better world look like? How do you convince others not only that your path forward will achieve success, but also that your idea of success aligns with their ideas? Unlike in times past, citizen statespeople today can't only fashion themselves as agents of progress; they need to be able to imagine what progress looks like in the first place, envision a future that aligns with that image, and enlist others in that vision before they begin to take action to make it real.

There is good news: first, the lack of a clear global direction gives citizen statespeople more freedom to choose a path that aligns with their own moral center and civic sensibilities. While that reality is daunting, it's also exciting, and offers a citizen statesperson a greater degree of latitude and self-expression than ever before. Where previously citizen statespeople only had control over the process they used to reach society's shared goals, today's citizen statespeople have agency when it comes to the goals themselves.

Second, the impact of all this disruption provides new opportunities for citizen statespeople to step to the forefront of the conversation and make a real and enduring impact. With less clear, undisputed, traditional leadership from respected institutions, individual citizen statespeople have the ability to make their own voices heard, and serve as citizen leaders with gravitas and authority. At a time of uncertainty, people might be more receptive to new and creative approaches for tackling stubborn and evolving issues.

Here's the bottom line: in moments of disarray, the citizen statesperson has an obligation and an opportunity to provide a beacon—to point the way forward, and to play a constructive role in furthering fundamental values.

Especially when traditional actors and institutions are not cooperating effectively together, it is vital for individuals in general, and for citizen statespeople in particular, to help fill the void.

Technology and the Citizen Statesperson

The world has changed in enormous ways both politically and socio-economically since the Second World War, but it has also changed technologically. Groundbreaking inventions alter the way we interact with one another and the environment around us. It seems that the pace of change is accelerating.

Here's the thing: the speed of those technological breakthroughs doesn't just *feel* as if it has grown. It is *actually* growing faster. In the first 171 years of its existence since it was founded in 1790, the U.S. Patent Office granted 3.3 million patents. After the semiconductor was invented in 1961, the Patent Office took just 38 years to grant 3.3 million more.[2] Technology builds on itself and generates exponential new opportunities. From the personal computer to the mobile phone to the Internet, we have seen entire industries rise and expand in the last few decades, creating new ways to live, work, and communicate.

Technological innovation has impacted on a global scale. Today, the world is more interconnected and interdependent than ever before. Information travels faster. News cycles have shortened. As a result, change at a micro level seems to occur more quickly—which drives more rapid change at a societal level as well.

The role of the citizen statesperson in this context is to help people understand the changes they're experiencing and help lead those changes in constructive ways. With change moving quicker and becoming more fluid, there is greater opportunity for individuals looking to engage in the process and take leadership roles to put their mark on the world.

More than at any time in history, individuals have the ability to learn, to connect, to launch movements, and to make changes that are seen, shared, and adopted by millions of people around the world.

Gaining Knowledge

Today, technology enables citizen statespeople to learn about causes and opportunities in ways unimaginable a generation ago, when most efforts to cultivate leadership arrived through word of mouth and concentric circles of personal relationships. Our age's citizen statespeople communicate as bloggers, TED talkers, YouTube channel managers, GoFundMe campaigners who raise money for local or global causes, self-published book authors, and more. If being a citizen statesperson is, in part, about finding opportunities and connecting dots to create personal and professional impact, then citizen statespeople enjoy better access to the tools of their trade than they've ever had.

A range of technologies is helping to make all this possible. To gain information quickly and from a wide array of sources, citizen statespeople turn to online resources like news publications, journals, message boards, and newsletters from well-respected institutions. These resources are often available at little or no cost, providing a useful pathway for citizen statespeople with financial constraints. Individuals can also consider subscribing to paid news and other sources for a fee. The fact that these resources can be accessed from anywhere with Internet connection means that the citizen statesperson can learn at his or her convenience, pace, and on his or her time.

Forging Connections

While the Internet provides entry to a virtual world of information, it can also offer a way into targeted communication and networking opportunities. Individuals who share your interests or have expertise in your field might live across the world, with little chance for in-person meetings. In the past, you might have had to interact impersonally—by mail, or later by telephone or email. But communication through written methods can sometimes come across slow and stilted, and phone conversations can hide physical cues and emotions and mask important body language. That's where virtual meetings make a real and important difference. Using remote video calls to discuss important topics with individuals in your field of interest can help you forge a closer connection, one-on-one or in small groups.

For a broader impact, you might turn to another form of technology: social media. A wide variety of apps and platforms can serve as your soapbox and your meeting room, providing a gathering location for interested individuals and a megaphone to inform others and generate enthusiasm around a topic.

Is all technology equally valuable for every purpose? Absolutely not! Citizen statespeople need to be thoughtful and discerning about the tools they utilize to learn about and interact with the issues that matter to them. For example, a social media site like Facebook might be a useful platform to organize like-minded individuals, but it probably won't be a great place to find valuable, unbiased information about important topics. While technology has made information of all kinds more accessible, citizen statespeople still need to exercise judgment around how and when they apply information to the causes they care about.

The same holds true when it comes to forging connections through technology solutions like social media with a low barrier to entry. Social media might enable a citizen statesperson to gain followers and build a larger platform with a bigger audience, but because social media does little to no screening of users and participants, the quality of those connections might be relatively poor. That reality might mean individuals are less engaged in the cause and less helpful than a person with whom you have forged a one-on-one connection. It also translates into knowing less about each individual person connected with you and your interest area—and that association with some of them could potentially damage your reputation and hinder your movement. That's not to say that a citizen statesperson will avoid organizing using social media and other low-barrier platforms, but it does mean that citizen statespeople have their antennae up when connecting more closely with people they don't know.

Catalyzing Movements

The explosion of technology is also helping to democratize citizen statespersonship and is making it easier for individuals to forge their own paths independent of traditional power structures, such as wealth and family connections. Previously, lack of elite social standing might have posed a challenge to people attempting to amplify their voices and push for change, but in an age when information and mass communication tools like social media are largely accessible regardless of conventional status, technology allows the vast majority of people to step beyond personal relationships alone and gain access to a broader array of opportunities. That's not to say that wealth and social status do not offer benefits. But the days of societal impact being available only to the well-off or the well-connected are clearly at an end.

The effectiveness of online, independent advocacy was clear during the Black Lives Matter movement. In 2013, Black Lives Matter began as a response to the acquittal of George Zimmerman, the suspect in Trayvon Martin's murder. After the death of Mike Brown in Ferguson, Missouri, the hashtag #blacklivesmatter grew as an organizing and mobilizing tool. Today, Black Lives Matter is an extensive organization with dozens of chapters around the country and a strong presence both online and in the physical world.

We saw a similar impact from the #MeToo movement. In 2006, sexual harassment survivor and activist Tarana Burke used the phrase "Me Too" to speak out about the prevalence of sexual abuse and other sexual crimes. After a raft of sexual abuse allegations against Harvey Weinstein became public in 2017, the phrase was adopted as a hashtag on Twitter, spreading throughout the English-speaking world and making its way into dozens of other languages. From the film industry to the sports industry to the military to politics and government and beyond, the amplification of #MeToo created a profound shift in how we talk about and ensure accountability for sexual crimes and harassment.

Transforming Lives

Of course, technology doesn't just make it easier for citizen statespeople to connect, to learn, and to grow. Technology is also pivotal to many of the solutions that are improving lives for people around the planet. At the International Maize and Wheat Improvement Center in Mexico, researchers and staff members are working to create new and more resilient kinds of maize that stand up to extreme weather conditions, like severe heat and lack of water. Countries like Tanzania, Morocco, and Ethiopia are using digital technologies like mobile money to connect poor and unbanked individuals with financial services—a transformation that helps people in remote areas participate in the local and national economy. Nations and organizations seeking to improve sanitation and save lives are developing reinvented toilets—affordable, self-contained lavatories that eliminate pathogens and turn human waste into valuable resources. From health to education, and from conservation to financial inclusion, technology is pushing the boundaries of what we once believed was possible, opening doors for citizen statespeople to get involved with new and exciting projects.

Consider Ryan Gersava's story. Born in Sultan Kudarat in the Philippines, and growing up poor as one of 11 children, Ryan learned the value of working hard in school. Ryan's academic achievements helped him earn a spot to study medicine at a local university—but when he found out he had hepatitis B during his first year in college, his dreams came to a screeching halt. He was told that his diagnosis meant he couldn't progress in the medical field and couldn't get a job as a medical technician—the role he had been seeking for years.

Ryan was devastated, but his experience also attuned him to the challenges faced by thousands of other Filipinos excluded from society—not only because of prejudice around medical issues like his, but because of related stigma around disabilities, drug history, incarceration history, and other challenges. He started thinking more broadly about how people who had been left out and left behind could find impactful new roles. And he developed a novel idea.

Ryan recognized that while local tech markets often excluded people with disabilities, there was strong demand for technically proficient workers from North American and European multinational companies. So, alongside his siblings, Ryan established Virtualahan, an organization that provides technical training and life coaching for people who typically face discrimination because of their current conditions or their former life, and helps them find online roles with companies overseas.

With four weeks of skills training, two weeks of on-the-job training, and three months of employment support and job coaching, Virtualahan seeks to help participants become financially and emotionally independent and develop support networks among their peers. Five years after it began, the organization boasts more than 600 alumni, a 98 percent completion rate, and a 78 percent employment rate among graduates—many of whom come from populations that would typically experience unemployment rates as high as 80 percent. Today, Ryan is working with big organizations in the United States, Sri Lanka, Germany, and other nations to hire Virtualahan's students or model programs like it in their own countries.

Ryan didn't originally have a background in technology. He had expected to use his skills in the medical field, and to work in a laboratory performing tests and assisting with medical diagnoses. Only after his own diagnosis did he begin to explore other options. Because he stayed open-minded, he was able to see other options not only for himself, but for countless other people in his community. Ryan recognized that, while the populations he served might not be in high demand locally, there was an international need that he could help fill. And he was able to harness online opportunities for himself and for others to gain proficiency and purpose.

Technology can also help scale solutions by decreasing the cost of infrastructure with massive social benefits. Water treatment facilities can provide communities with clean water, reducing health risks and allowing residents to live longer, more productive lives. Broadband access can connect rural towns and outposts with education resources and economic opportunities that might otherwise pass them by. Electrification of public transportation can bring social and economic benefits to all sorts of neighborhoods while reducing carbon emissions.

Over time, these technologies are becoming more pervasive, more sophisticated, cheaper, and more accessible. In some cases, inventors and developers are learning how to produce sophisticated products with more cost-effective components and materials. In other examples, complex systems are being mass-produced, making them more readily available to the public. As cost-effective technologies offer new solutions, citizen statespeople will find ways to connect solutions to communities at the local level where they drive the greatest impact.

Spurring Revolutions

Remember, this is just the beginning. Just as the number of U.S. patents grew exponentially after the invention of the semiconductor, so too will new technologies and ideas proliferate as time goes on. The technologies that separate the present from past moments are social media, the Internet, and mobile connectedness. Technological changes that are likely to impact the next generation of citizen statespeople will include 5G networks, quantum computing, AI, accessible supersonic travel, and technologies we cannot yet fathom.

Imagine, for a moment, what the world might look like in the next generation. We may be able to connect seamlessly to every person around the world, creating a truly global network that allows a citizen statesperson to communicate with anyone at any time. We may be able to physically travel enormous distances in short times, incalculably strengthening our relationships with our peers and allies. We may be able to obtain opportunities that might never have been available before, or we may be able to take part in experiences that would previously have remained out of reach.

Ultimately, serving as a citizen statesperson is not static, because the world is not static. We will continue to see adjustments in the geopolitical atmosphere and in how we relate to it. Just as a citizen statesperson must be strong enough to set a path through an uncertain global climate, one must also be flexible enough to connect continually with an ever-changing world.

Discussion Questions

- What does "progress" look like to you? What does your vision of a better world entail?
- How will your current use of technology help you gain useful information, make connections, and build a movement for impact?
- What steps do you need to take to harness the power of technology and grow your impact as a citizen statesperson?

Notes

1. Freedom House, "Freedom in the World 2019: Democracy in Retreat," 2019, https://freedomhouse.org/report/freedom-world/2019/democracy-retreat.
2. The Atlantic and Prudential, "How Fast Is Technology Accelerating?" Atlantic Re:think, https://www.theatlantic.com/sponsored/prudential-great-expectations/how-fast-is-technology-accelerating/360/.

5

You Can Do It

Key Takeaways
- The Millennial generation is uniquely suited to citizen statespersonship.
- Aspiring citizen statespeople need to frame their role in a way that enables focus, action, and confidence.
- Firsthand experience offers useful insights for building impactful solutions.

MILLENNIALS MAY BE the first full generation of citizen statespeople. That may feel surprising, because a widespread existing—and misguided—impression of Millennials characterizes them as shallow, disengaged, and disinterested in difficult work. Millennials, so the stereotype suggests, insist on immediate and constant feedback. This portrayal also holds that they are so independently minded that they lack deep roots in community, and that they avoid traditional indicators of connection like developing roots in a community, getting married, and buying a home. In some cases, Millennials are viewed as existing in a period of prolonged adolescence, preferring to remain with their parents rather than make their way in the world. According to detractors, Millennials are more likely to tweet or post on TikTok about an issue or grievance than to put in the hard, sustained effort to make a change.

Some of these skewed stereotypes find their roots in data. According to a 2019 study from the Pew Research Center, Millennials are delaying traditional milestones like marriage and buying a home.[1] They are slower in forming their own households, and they are more likely than previous generations to live at home with their parents, and for longer stretches.

Yet Millennials as a generation broadly share characteristics that well equip and position them to serve as effective citizen statespeople. In general, Millennials are better-educated than the generations before them. As of 2018, nearly 40 percent of Millennials held a bachelor's degree or higher—a sharp increase from the fewer than 30 percent of Gen X-ers who had completed some form of higher education at the same age, and the 25 percent of Baby Boomers who had done the same.

The data are especially striking for women in the Millennial generation. In 2018, 43 percent of Millennial women had received a bachelor's degree or higher, marking only the second successive generation in which women are better-educated than men. Millennial women are also more likely to join the workforce than their peers in prior generations, offering more financial independence and gender parity than ever before.

Millennials' experiences have primed them to recognize economic inequality. As a result of the Great Recession that began in 2007, Millennials in general faced significant challenges to entering the workforce and beginning their careers. Lack of jobs meant lower salaries for those who did find employment. The rising cost of college tuition also led to rising levels of student debt. Ultimately, a combination of these factors has coalesced to make it more difficult for Millennials to build wealth, resulting in a lower median net worth than Gen X-ers and Boomers had at the same age.

At the same time, Millennials' demographics enable them to better identify and respond to racial injustice. The generation is more diverse than any in recent memory; just over half is characterized as "non-Hispanic White." Meanwhile, shifting attitudes, driven by young people, have led to an increase in racial and ethnic intermarriages, giving more people a personal stake in racial justice issues.

We've seen this kind of effort take shape in advocacy organizations like the Sunrise Movement, which fights for action to address climate change; March for Our Lives, which included the largest single day of protest against gun violence in history; and United We Dream, which brought young undocumented immigrants together to demand protections for Dreamers—undocumented immigrants who had been brought to the United States as children and were in danger of being deported. From the drive for a $15 minimum wage, known as the Fight for $15 movement, to Black Lives Matter, Millennials have been at the center of building recent large-scale campaigns for change.

Millennials have also grown up during a time when methods of communication and connection have become more widespread, from the prevalence of personal computers and the Internet to the explosion in cell phone use and social media. Those phenomena—the multiplication of communication channels and the democratization of information—have helped lower barriers to knowledge. As information has become more accessible, expertise has become more attainable, making traditional credentials less important than a generation ago.

Make Yourself an Expert

That is not to say that substance and experience don't matter. They do! Speaking in an authoritative tone is not the same as speaking with authority, and confidence isn't the same as knowledge. Passing yourself off as an expert certainly isn't the same as building real expertise. The point is that it's possible to become a subject-matter expert on a topic—or at least, to become a meaningful part of the conversation—without an extensive formal education or a 20-year career in a related industry.

Here's an example: when Chelsea Collier was growing up, there wasn't a strong movement around the idea of "smart cities"— communities and urban areas that employ electronic methods and sensors to collect data in order to improve operations around the city. She went to the University of Texas in the 1990s, and graduated with a bachelor's and later a master's degree in advertising. But as time went on, information about how technology could be used to improve city living became more attainable. Opportunities that would allow her to explore her interests became more accessible. And she connected with other individuals interested in making a difference.

By 2013, she had become a vice chair of the Austin Community Technology and Telecommunications Commission, working to create a digitally inclusive community in the Greater Austin area. By 2016, she was an advisor to the Austin Technology Alliance—a nonpartisan nonprofit promoting civic engagement in Austin's tech sector. Later that year, she founded Digi.City to provide information and host events that advance the conversation around smart city policy and programs, and became an editor-at-large at Smart Cities Connect—a forum designed to empower smart cities at all stages of growth.

Collier's course of formal study didn't put her on the path to a career in smart cities. Instead, her commitment to the cause, her interest in the subject, and her motivation to conduct her own learning and gain her own experience allowed her to blaze a trail forward. That was made possible by new methods of connection, communication, and learning that offer open access to expertise.

Recognize What You Bring to the Table

We get it: jumping into citizen statespersonship is scary. But remember, characteristics that fuel insecurities can also serve as strengths. Are you inexperienced? Maybe! But your fresh perspective can be valuable in some of the fastest-moving, most impactful areas of social change. Are you feeling reticent? Perhaps! But that just means that you're challenging yourself, and doing something worthy of your time and energy. Are you facing scrutiny from other stakeholders or organizations? Sure! But learning how to navigate the existing power structure or hierarchy in your field of interest will mold you into a much more effective problem-solver.

Let's consider an example. Health access is a critical challenge for many populations across the United States. Many communities suffer from a lack of trust in the medical establishment. In some communities—and particularly in communities of color—that mistrust is rooted in a history of racism in American medicine, from the infamous Tuskegee Syphilis Study that withheld treatment from Black Americans, to more recent studies showing that Black Americans have consistently been undertreated for pain in comparison with White patients.[2] In other communities, including rural neighborhoods, avoidance might be due to barriers like stigma and a lack of culturally appropriate interventions.[3] This lack of trust and healthcare avoidance, among other factors, contribute to a wide gap in health outcomes.

If you're interested in exploring this topic, you might want to engage with the people and groups that work to improve health access. So who's focused on these issues? Who has the knowledge and expertise? There are experts who have spent decades studying medicine, hospital systems, and healthcare distribution. There are think tanks and organizations with vast stores of information about the differences between rates of health screenings, vaccinations, and health outcomes among populations and communities. There are advocacy organizations devoted to learning about the topic and pushing policymakers to engage with the issue in a meaningful way. There are real people in real communities who are struggling.

Do you fit into one of those categories? Maybe not. But there may also be room for young people who have their fingers on the pulse of how we receive knowledge, how we develop skepticism, how we hone the tools that allow us to filter information, and whom we trust to give us suggestions and instructions when it comes to our own health and well-being.

You might not be a healthcare expert. You might not have written scholarly papers or well-read books on the subject. But you could be extremely well positioned to communicate with affected populations and connect communities with the resources they need. Do you come from a neighborhood that might be impacted by challenges around healthcare access? Are you familiar with the institutions that are trusted among members of the community—from religious leaders to barbers to neighbors in the medical field? Are you well versed in the methods that your community uses to communicate, whether they involve online interactions or regular in-person gatherings or events?

To many aspiring citizen statespeople, familiarity with these topics might not immediately seem like subject-area expertise. It doesn't come from years of scholarship or careful study or traditional investments of time and training. But the truth is that your background and real-world knowledge might be invaluable in solving clear and intractable challenges. Maybe you can organize a network of trusted authorities within the community that encourages people to schedule health screenings or get vaccinations. Maybe you can develop an online effort through a local social media group to provide useful information about healthcare options. Maybe you can offer to be a connector for a traditional expert in the field, contributing your practical knowledge alongside their policy proficiency to design effective models for health access at scale.

In fact, simply being a member of an impacted community can help a citizen statesperson identify critical challenges and work to build important solutions. That's something Karim Abouelnaga learned firsthand.

Karim, whose Egyptian father died when he was age 13, grew up in Queens, New York, as one of seven children raised in poverty by a single mother. Karim didn't realize the value of an education until he was a teenager; as someone whose family struggled to pay the bills and keep their heads above water, he was less concerned about his next class than about his next meal. Consequently, he struggled in school. In seventh grade, he was absent for a full 60 days.

Over time, though, Karim stemmed the slide, reengaged in his schoolwork, and earned over $300,000 in aid and scholarships to attend Cornell University. Based on his own experience as a poor kid struggling to keep up, he was inspired to start Practice Makes Perfect, a program designed to help underserved young people learn.

One of the biggest problems, he says, is that students from low-income areas regress in the summer, losing two to three months of learning compared to more affluent students. When kids from low-income areas return to school, teachers spend two months reteaching old material. That means these students lose five months of learning: half of a ten-month school year.

Practice Makes Perfect emerged from that understanding as a K-8 summer enrichment program that helps train teachers to become coaches, enlists older students as paid mentors to fund their college education, and aims to get all students engaged in what and how they're learning. Each summer, Practice Makes Perfect supports 500-plus students from New York City schools. So far, Karim's evaluations have shown that students who take part are making gains of around one month's worth of learning in math and two months' worth of learning in reading.

Could a person with more experience in education policy have designed a program like that? Maybe. But it's clear that Karim's lived experience helped him recognize what underserved students were facing, and provided insights into how a new program could meet their needs.

That's the kind of awareness a citizen statesperson needs to recognize his or her value and create real and effective change.

No matter who you are or where you come from, it's likely that you possess an important, useful perspective that could be applied to a larger opportunity.

If you're like Karim, you might use your unique insight to design an education program. In the health access example, you might leverage your background into a role with a large and respected healthcare company seeking to expand into rural communities, or pitch yourself to a think tank or activist organization as a potential leader in grassroots advocacy. Whatever the opportunity you're seeking, you have a vital perspective and a useful skill set.

In some cases, youth itself is an asset. Margo Jordan started her own organization at just 26 years old. Growing up in Milwaukee, Margo had seen many peers face tough issues, from suicide to teen pregnancy to bullying and violence. It hadn't been easy to find positive role models and experiences. And so, after a stint in the U.S. Army and an education at Texas Southern University, Margo created "Chicks with Class"—a tween empowerment group that focused on young people in underserved communities.

Margo's firsthand experience helped forge programming that encouraged tweens and teens to gain self-confidence, learn social skills, and develop a healthy sense of self-worth. With annual conferences as well as workshops around confidence and self-esteem, Chicks with Class empowers young people to see the best in themselves and each other. Through drop-in learning and etiquette programs, they build social skills and highlight character education. Birthday parties and summer camp workshops enable participants to connect with other young people in positive environments.

In the years since she created Chicks with Class, Margo expanded her work by founding Youth Enrichments, a public-benefit corporation that offers digital programs and workshops around self-esteem, social skills, and mental health, as well as live content with tween and teen influencers. Rather than leaving her unprepared to build an organization, her age and lived experiences made her uniquely aware of what young people needed—and uniquely able to deliver it.

This isn't just a bunch of feel-good happy talk. It's part of a necessary process to get your head in the game and make sure you're contributing to the best of your ability.

That's important, because our world needs you to step up to fulfill your potential, and you don't need an invitation to participate.

> *Don't weed yourself out. Instead, give yourself permission to become an expert—when you believe in yourself, other people will believe in you, too.*

Okay, we hear you ask. *But how do you know if you're offering a fresh perspective, or if you just have a lack of fundamental knowledge? How do you know whether you're bravely throwing yourself at big opportunities, or futilely pushing yourself towards out-of-reach prospects?*

Those are great questions that we as co-authors answer differently. Dean's basic assessment is that leaders and citizen statespeople are intrepid by nature. His instinct is to uncover opportunities that have never been available; to scale heights that have never been conquered; and to achieve distinctions that have never existed before. That often comes with a certain degree of discomfort, but his view is that if you're curious, creative, and motivated, a lack of traditional experience is immaterial. As long as you have the will to engage, and approach opportunities with earnestness and a readiness to learn and contribute, people will recognize your leadership potential. You may not be a subject matter expert to begin with, but if you push yourself and do your homework, there's no reason why you can't contribute at the highest levels. Maybe you'll throw yourself into the deep end so many times that you'll find the bottom of the pool—but the important thing is to remain undeterred.

Dean also emphasizes what he calls the "Law of Other." The Law of Other suggests that every person is made up of a range of different skills and identities that can be seen as distinct from one another. In any given situation it's worthwhile to be able to emphasize whichever identity sets you apart from the group. By casting yourself as someone who is "other," you provide an expertise and a lived experience that is rare and potentially useful.

Here's an example: Dean is a practicing attorney with an international focus, but he's also someone deeply involved with policy and political interests. Those could be seen as two separate identities. Understanding that reality, Dean might choose to emphasize one identity over the other, depending on the situation. If he's meeting with a group of policymakers or politicians, he can present himself as someone with experience in international law and business. If he's in a room full of international lawyers, his political and policy chops set him apart and make him valuable in a way distinguished from the group. Either way, he's memorable within the group, and offers expertise that is a distinct value-add from the people around him.

You can apply that "Law of Other" principle to guide your path. If you're not traditionally qualified for a position or an opportunity, think of a trait or part of your background that would position you as a strong out-of-the-box choice, or an interesting addition to the team—then make the case for why someone like you should be considered. That's also why it's useful to cultivate a wide variety of different experiences; the more expansive your interests, and the broader your portfolio of causes and projects, the wider your selection of applicable talents.

Carrie has a slightly different, but not contradictory, way of thinking about the challenge. Her view is that there's value to a methodical approach that finds the edges of your comfort zone and the contours of your abilities. Rather than going from zero to

100, find a smaller platform or a more achievable objective that allows you to demonstrate citizen statespersonship in a way that seems realistic to you. Search for extraordinary opportunities that you feel qualified to take on. Trying to make a difference in a smaller setting will help build confidence that you can do it in a bigger one.

Recently, Carrie joined the board of directors of a large, $20 billion organization. That was a new experience for her because she had previously been involved primarily with smaller organizations where the dynamics were different. She wasn't sure if her experience would translate well to the new role, or if she would find herself out of place. In this context, it would have been easy for her to decide that she didn't have the requisite expertise in this area, or that she wasn't qualified to participate.

Instead, she prepared for the role. Carrie spoke with people she sees as coaches and mentors, especially those with corporate board experience, and asked them to help her understand how her thinking would be relevant in this larger setting. They were encouraging and informative, and it was helpful to have people who understood the opportunity and understood Carrie to help her connect the dots. Ultimately, they helped her understand how her approach to citizen statespersonship could be relevant no matter the scale of the opportunity, and how the principles of good leadership could be just as effective in a large corporate setting as they were in a smaller organization.

Carrie also used the interview process to test the existing board's receptivity to her fresh perspective. That meant expressing her views, and assessing whether her approach would be welcome in the room. She wasn't interested in participating if "participating" simply meant sitting on the sidelines; instead, she wanted to enter an environment where people would engage with her ideas and be open to a dynamic conversation. Ultimately, she used a practical, methodical approach to gauge her suitability for the role, and to ensure that the organization was a good fit for her.

Again, you may ask: *How do you know whether you're bravely throwing yourself at big opportunities, or futilely tilting at out-of-reach windmills?* Maybe the best way to think about this question, then, is by using an amalgam of Dean's and Carrie's approaches. Take big swings, and consider building self-assurance and experience along the way. Push your limits, and try to explore the edges of your comfort zone. If you're finding a stream of constant rejections difficult to endure, or if being rebuffed repeatedly is making you question your self-worth, take a step back and consider an opportunity that you feel more confident about. But don't put artificial limits on yourself, or avoid stimulating opportunities because you're afraid of being dismissed.

Keep in mind that nobody looks at a successful person's resume and says, "There's a person who failed." Most high achievers are rejected more often than they're accepted. The important thing is to keep pushing forward, to keep reaching for exciting goals, to keep trusting your abilities, and to keep working towards fulfilling opportunities.

Here's a tip: surround yourself with good people. If you're hearing from detractors every step of the way, you'll have a hard time making progress. If you are supported by people who build you up and offer solutions, they will help you feel confident and promote your success. That's something we know from experience.

Develop Your Expertise

Once you've given yourself permission to develop expertise on your road to citizen statespersonship, continue to educate yourself on an issue and gain substance on a topic. There are plenty of ways to do that, from reading available news and studies to speaking with experts to engaging with impacted individuals and communities. That process might seem overwhelming at first—there's a lot of information!—but remember: the process of becoming an expert is about taking one step at a time. Nobody expects you to become an authority overnight. Spend time each day looking for opportunities to learn from people and organizations with relevant information.

First, see what you can learn from public sources. Begin by reading relevant journalism or a newspaper of record to survey what's been written about a topic. Read journals or listen to podcasts that deal with the concept in more detail. On any given issue, identify which organizations are being mentioned most frequently. If there are think tanks or advocacy groups involved, go to their websites to explore their talking points and dive into their research.

Next, go an additional step by connecting directly with knowledgeable individuals. Who do public sources cite as the major players in the field? Who are the people most often quoted or mentioned in stories or public resources about the topic you care about? If there are organizations doing significant work in the area, try to get in touch with their leaders by requesting a conversation. You might be surprised by how often you'll hear back, and how valuable your interest will be.

When Dean was a 20-something graduate student, he went to a book signing in order to meet George Mitchell, who had served as a U.S. senator and diplomat who played a leading role in negotiations for peace in Northern Ireland. Dean was determined to use the opportunity to ask Senator Mitchell a question about leadership and diplomacy—and when he finally approached Mitchell, he did exactly that.

Years later, after Dean had gone on to become a lawyer, he ended up working at a global law firm chaired by none other than George Mitchell. When Dean had an opportunity to work with Mitchell on a project, he made sure to note that they had actually met before.

"You won't remember me," said Dean, "but years ago, I cornered you in a bookstore to ask you a question."

"Of course!" said Mitchell. Not only did he remember meeting Dean—he remembered the question Dean asked.

That story says a lot about Mitchell's impressive memory, but it also speaks to the value of earnest interest in an issue, and the willingness to ask questions of knowledgeable individuals. The reality is that experts are experts for a reason; they're interested in the topics they study and are generally enthusiastic about sharing their knowledge. If you approach experts with respect and with a genuine desire to learn, you may be surprised by how willing they are to connect.

Of course, you don't have to interact with the foremost expert in the field in order to learn. If you can't connect with a renowned leader or a celebrated authority, reach out to a policy director at a think tank, or a researcher, or an advocate. Anyone who knows more than you do will be able to expand your knowledge base and improve your understanding of the topic.

At the end of your conversation, ask these individuals for recommendations for your next informational conversation. If you're able to secure a quick coffee or a phone conversation—or even a five-minute chat—with a knowledgeable individual, make sure you ask them if there is another person whose thinking they respect in the space, or if there's an article or book or podcast they would recommend to someone who's interested in learning more. Learning is like using stepping-stones to cross a river; rather than trying to jump over the entire stream in one superhuman bound, think about hopping from your current stone to the next stone. Every step forward matters, and every individual stone will help move you to the other side.

Gathering information from experts is important, but you also want to be a critical thinker. Give yourself an opportunity to ask questions about the information you're receiving. What is the background or motivation of the person or organization providing you with information? What is their bias or agenda? Why does their information matter? What questions are not being asked, or asked the wrong way, or to the wrong people? What other individuals are worth contacting, or who might have an important view?

This last question is especially important, because it can help guide your next moves as you broaden your thinking and sharpen your approach. For example, if you're interested in reducing pollution, you might learn from experts about regulations that limit methane emissions. That's an important issue—but it's also one that has a dramatic impact on farming and agriculture. So ask yourself: is there someone along that supply chain who would be impacted by a regulation limiting methane? How would you find a person like that? How might you gain their perspective in order to build a more comprehensive view of the challenge at hand?

The same principle holds true for all sorts of issue areas. If you want to learn more about healthcare policy, see if you can speak to scholars and experts as well as individuals who have been impacted by the current system. If you're interested in immigration, read about deportation policies and also speak to Dreamers, DACA recipients, and border patrol officials. In every scenario, consider whether there is a person who has been impacted by the issue in a tangible way, and then connect with that person to listen and learn.

One benefit of this strategy is that people closer to the ground may be more accessible than well-known experts. It may be easier to connect with an individual who lives out of the public eye than with a giant in the field who receives hundreds of invitations and meeting requests every week. But it also provides you with a valuable and rare tool that you can deploy as you scope opportunities to make change. If you find yourself in a conversation or making a connection with a politician or a professor who you feel might otherwise dismiss you as inexperienced or uninformed, give them the benefit of your interpersonal experiences, and convey what you've learned from individuals on the ground. That approach demonstrates your authenticity and credibility, and arms you with new and useful perspectives to offer big thinkers.

Speaking of new perspectives, remember that the world is not a static place. We live in incredibly dynamic times. Part of the learning process must be considering how to apply a new lens to existing challenges. Has changing technology or shifting social standards or practices changed the game or provided a fresh way to look at an issue? Is there a way to consider the world through a filter that better reflects the current moment?

Asking these questions won't necessarily help you cook up a grand new theory that changes everybody's view, but it might help you consider how to be of service, and how to make yourself useful to a world that needs your help.

Connect in Meaningful Ways

Consider how to stay focused on the issues you care about in ways that help you gather momentum as a citizen statesperson. You may gain a foothold by writing an article or a blog, planning an event, or participating in a podcast. Over time, you'll want to make concrete progress, whether that involves fundraising through a nonprofit, advocating to pass a piece of legislation, or convincing elected officials to focus on an issue you care about. In the meantime, you'll want to get your foot in the door and get in the room.

Here's tactical, practical advice: When people offer a seat at the table, take it. That's not as simple as it sounds; all sorts of insecurities tend to stop us from taking the opportunities we're offered to be a part of the conversation. Whether we're plagued by impostor syndrome or just temporarily surprised by an offer, it can be easy to step back instead of stepping up. So make sure that you seize your invitation or opening to engage.

Don't stop there. Once you have a seat, use your voice. Speak up when you have something valuable to contribute. You're present for a reason, so don't fade into the background.

That advice comes from experience. As a young lawyer, Dean was asked to attend a phone conference on a topic for which he was not an expert. The other participants were more experienced, more knowledgeable, and more senior, and Dean wasn't sure what he could possibly contribute.

Dean remembered hearing this advice:

When you don't have an expert opinion, recap and summarize what you've heard so everyone aligns on the path forward. That kind of action has real value, because it helps everyone take a step back, synthesize the situation, and understand the central issue.

So Dean gave it a shot—and the moment he did, the senior law partner in the room hit the mute button, leaned over to Dean, and said, "Congratulations—you just earned your seat at the table."

That was Dean's aha moment.

There's an old aphorism that says it is better to remain silent and be thought a fool than to speak and to remove all doubt. People have a natural reticence to think, "If this topic is not my strongest area, it would be better to not say anything at all." The problem with that approach is that when you stay silent, you erode the rationale for your presence at the table. Why are you there, if you're not going to participate? Instead, find a way to contribute to the conversation.

There are plenty of ways to do that. You can recap the situation or take people back to first principles to remind everyone what you're trying to accomplish. You can reframe what's being asked in order to find a new angle. You can make a comparison to another experience to help participants think about the topic in a new way—for example, *I know that when we saw such and such unfold, we thought about it like this. How would that apply in our current situation?* Push yourself to say something at every meeting in order to validate your presence.

That's also the advice Carrie received from her boss early in her career: to offer at least one comment every time she was invited to a meeting. If she was in a conversation, she was there on purpose and for a reason, and that meant she had something valuable to contribute—whether or not she knew it.

Putting that advice into practice wasn't comfortable. During weekly executive meetings, Carrie sat in the board meeting room with colleagues—all but one of them men—who were 40 to 50 years her senior. It was an intimidating setting. But in every meeting, Carrie forced herself to make a comment or raise a question. Over time, that experience solidified her position as a valuable contributor in the overall conversation and at the table itself. In fact, in one meeting after she had been actively participating for some weeks, Carrie arrived at the board room to find that there were too many people in attendance to fit comfortably around the table. Quickly recognizing that she was the most junior colleague present, Carrie began to move her chair back in order to make room for others. But before she could take a seat, the most senior individual in the room pulled a chair to his side and said, "Come, take your seat at the table."

That's an important lesson: When you consistently make yourself part of the conversation, you earn a consistent seat at the table.

Now, that's all well and good—but what if you haven't been invited to the meeting? What if you haven't been offered an opportunity to get involved? Or what if you still don't feel able to contribute to the conversation?

The reality is that there are plenty of ways to get started in an area that matters to you—even if you don't feel ready to jump in with both feet. Help to organize meetings on a topic you care about in order to meet people where they are. Offer to help with projects that aren't assigned. There's almost always room

Help edit if you're not ready to write. Help research if you're not ready to publish. Take and share pictures if you're not ready to be the content.

within organizations and existing movements for people who want to provide organizational support.

When someone in your network is busy and doesn't have time to deliver on logistics, volunteer to be the person who helps complete the task. You will go from relative anonymity to the person who helps run the show. Everyone needs a partner who's actually going to deliver.

The most important players in every team are usually stretched thin, overcommitted, and under-resourced. This gap creates an opportunity. If you offer your energy, your time, and your skills to fill that gap, you can build durable relationships and become indispensable to an organization. Think of yourself like a de facto chief of staff—someone who sees a 30,000-foot view of the team, who can understand how decisions are made at the highest level, and who can be a repository for valuable institutional knowledge. Some organizations might not realize they need a chief of staff, but thinking like one can help you rise within an organization. And eventually, you'll be qualified to do the job.

That word—*eventually*—is important. Once you do the homework and get engaged, give yourself time for your efforts to reach fruition. It's natural to be impatient, but change can take time, and it doesn't often happen on our own schedule. You can create the conditions and introduce a catalyst for change, but there will frequently be factors outside of your control that determine the timing for change to emerge.

With that in mind, think about short-term goals that can help mark your progress. Climate change and homelessness are major issues that require long-term systemic change. Building a smart city or a workforce of the future is an enormous task. Making a change on these issues, and others like them, isn't like flipping a switch. Instead, you have to see each step forward as a victory. Engage one person, family, or community at a time—and build the momentum needed to eventually change the system or outcomes.

Defeat Impostor Syndrome

Just because the information is available doesn't mean it's easy to become an expert. In many instances, in fact, people who are interested in becoming citizen statespeople might be held back by their own anxiety.

That's called impostor syndrome.

Impostor syndrome can be frightening. It can make smart and motivated people feel like frauds—unqualified for their work and unable to make a difference. And in an ironic twist, it disproportionately affects high-achieving people.

Here's the thing: it's okay to carry a bit of impostor syndrome. Sure, it's scary and frustrating, and can make you worry about your ability to make an impact. Being purposeful is hard. To break new ground in your life, you have to do things that feel uncomfortable because they represent new terrain. If you can recognize that impostor syndrome is irrational, you can identify your internal barriers. You can understand what is prompting your concerns. And you can gently set aside the feeling that you are less than anyone else.

That can be as simple as giving yourself permission to become an expert without filtering yourself out or becoming your own voice of exclusion. Begin with the understanding that you have a lot to give; that your life experiences are valuable, and that you have the ability to provide context and new ideas to a topic where traditional experts and talking heads may fall short.

Don't give up. Don't get discouraged. You. Can. Do. It.

Discussion Questions
- What are your qualities and life experiences that would be useful in your field of interest?
- What are the gaps in your knowledge or expertise, and how can you compensate or fill those gaps?
- In what areas are you being too hard on yourself? Do you experience impostor syndrome, and if so, how can you overcome it?

Notes

1. Kristen Bialik and Richard Fry, "Millennial life: How young adulthood today compares with prior generations," Pew Research Center, February 14, 2019, https://www.pewresearch.org/social-trends/2019/02/14/millennial-life-how-young-adulthood-today-compares-with-prior-generations-2/.
2. For example, see Salimah H. Meghani, Eeeseung Byun, and Rollin M. Gallagher, "Time to take stock: a meta-analysis and systemic review of analgesic treatment disparities for pain in the United States," *Pain Med* 13(2), 2012, 150–74, https://pubmed.ncbi.nlm.nih.gov/22239747/.
3. Angela M. Spleen et al., "Health Care Avoidance Among Rural Populations: Results From a Nationally Representative Survey," *Journal of Rural Health* 30(1), June 24, 2013, https://www.ncbi.nlm.nih.gov/pmc/articles/PMC3882339/.

6

Leveraging Established, Powerful Organizations to Create Positive Change

---

Key Takeaways

- To gain credibility, focus on truly connecting with people and establishing relationships.
- To gain insight, access pertinent resources and seek out different perspectives that reflect important considerations.
- To gain relevance, share your insight and broader perspective, keeping the focus on how you can support renewal in established organizations.

THERE'S A SCHOOL of thought that suggests change can only come from the outside, that disruption is the key to progress, and that old, ossified institutions simply don't have the capacity or the will to generate leadership.

To that, we say: meh.

Look, it's certainly possible for impressive people to succeed by thumbing their noses at the establishment and refusing to be a part of existing power structures. Styling yourself as a revolutionary with no connections to the elite may be an appealing approach, and there's no doubt that fresh ideas and unique strategies are important to problem-solving. Building your own power base outside of mainstream organizations also gives you more freedom and flexibility. But ignoring or actively avoiding interactions with established institutions that hold sway in your field of interest also prevents you from enjoying the benefits and opportunities that those institutions offer.

Let's consider what some of those benefits might be. Established institutions might be able to provide useful expertise or insights about current industry thinking. They might offer forums for meeting other citizen statespeople with shared interests. An affiliation might lend you an aura of credibility, an opportunity to learn from thought leaders, or even a platform for generating and contributing thought leadership of your own.

While establishing deep connections with established institutions may not be the ultimate goal of a citizen statesperson, they are part of the journey. Don't fall for a false choice that suggests creating change requires going through established power structures or creating your own power base. If you approach them with an open mind and a sense of purpose, organizations like think tanks and NGOs can serve as the living, breathing universities of your civic life.

Let's dig deeper. Why, exactly, should citizen statespeople leverage established, powerful organizations?

Credibility

Let's say you're a health-focused entrepreneur. You go to a meeting or a forum on health policy at a leading think tank, and because you're at the think tank, other forum attendees might be inclined to connect with you as a serious person in the industry.

Now consider a different scenario: one in which you're the same person, with the same start-up business, but you contact a potential industry partner for the first time without the context of a meeting at the prominent think tank. You're likely to have a tougher time breaking through, and you will likely face higher barriers to entry.

Why?

We all know that it's not rocket science:

Introductions made without context are naturally met with a degree of skepticism, whereas connections that are made in the context of shared interests, and in a forum of substance and reputation, come with credibility.

Think of it like getting an introduction from an established executive as compared to navigating on your own. The introduction offers others a reference point and a framework to understand your actions, interests, and motives; lends you an aura of authority; and instantly makes you a more formidable citizen statesperson. Your mere presence in a setting where thought leadership takes place says that you are a part of the conversation and a contributor to the cause. That makes you someone worth knowing.

This reality came to pass for Carrie when she started building The Global Good Fund in collaboration with Knox Singleton, who was the then CEO of Inova Health System, a multibillion-dollar organization. Carrie was 25 years old, just getting started in her career. As co-founders of The Global Good Fund, Knox and Carrie's jobs were clear: Knox would open doors to high-powered people leading prominent organizations and Carrie would run through the open doors, asking individuals to give their time, network, talent, and financial resources. The strategy worked and that's how The Global Good Fund was born. Would it have taken longer to build The Global Good Fund without Knox's introductions? Unquestionably, yes. The individuals whom Knox introduced Carrie to for the sake of building the organization are hard to reach—there are intentional barriers to entry, like executive assistants and family office infrastructure. Knox already knew how to navigate those barriers. So when Carrie came philosophically and literally running through the door, the reaction of the other party was, "Gee, I wonder what this cause could be about that Knox found it so compelling, I think I'll listen." The individuals in this case who granted meetings are wonderful human beings; they are also busy and in high demand, so they need to be selective about how they spend their time. That's precisely why having introductions from an established executive mattered deeply in building The Global Good Fund.

Interestingly, once the peer-established executive took the meeting with Carrie, most of the time that individual made a referral to another high-powered person leading another established organization. This virtuous cycle of referrals has a ripple effect.

Another key factor to consider when building credibility is the power of place. The power of place is real. Be attuned to your setting when you decide where to make important connections. Think of it this way:

Think strategically about how to make the best use of that power of place. You might use it to enhance or draw attention to your existing expertise by participating in events that occur under the auspices of thought leadership organizations. You might use it to compensate for a perceived weakness in your background or resume; for example, if you're interested in foreign affairs

If we communicate through stories, and life is our theater, then the context in which we interact with people is the stage. Your goal is to set the stage as effectively as possible to convey your conviction and capability to effect change.

but you aren't traveling around the world yet, support to travel from an organization with geographic reach helps to create the assumption that you've been vetted. You might even use the offices or grounds of an established organization to meet with other like-minded individuals. Affiliations with long-standing, robust institutions help cultivate a public perception of resilience, staying power, and that you, the citizen statesperson, stand a greater chance of reaching the intended audience.

In some cases, the power of place may have consequences beyond your expectations. Recently, Carrie was involved in a phone conversation with Howard Kern, CEO of Sentara Health—a $6 billion healthcare organization in Virginia. The meeting resulted from an introduction by Barry Duval, CEO at the Richmond Chamber of Commerce, thanks to a previous introduction from The Global Good Fund's board member Fred Thompson.

In the midst of the phone call, Howard went quiet for a moment, then said, "I think we've met before. It was at the attorney general's office." It turned out that a decade previously, Carrie's then-boss and mentor, Knox, had brought her along to a meeting in Richmond, Virginia, with the state's attorney general, where he and other health CEOs were working to improve public health. As Carrie recalls, she wasn't central to the meeting; Knox had brought her as a mentoring opportunity, to let her witness how health policy was made. But the auspicious setting in the attorney general's office had made her memorable—to the point that another meeting participant remembered her ten years later, in the midst of a global pandemic, during a completely different conversation.

That's an example of how your presence in important institutions and settings can serve you and, ultimately, your cause as a citizen statesperson.

Of course, you don't have to wait for a person to remember you from years before; you can act proactively and use affiliation with an established institution to connect with other important stakeholders. You might attend events held by the organization where other citizen statespeople will be in the room—this strategy works in both physical and virtual settings. Ahead of the meeting, identify the people you want to connect with, and take the initiative to interact with them. However you choose to move forward, it's important to bear in mind that building credibility is not typically a quick or easy process—be prepared to follow up as needed.

That may mean connecting through multiple interactions. You could meet someone in person and get their contact information, or figure out how to connect through social media. You could place them on your radar for a time and send them articles or opportunities you think they'd appreciate. Perhaps they happen to mention that their daughter is interested in photography, and later coincidentally hear that there's a great photography exhibition coming to town. Send a note saying, "I thought you'd appreciate this event, given your daughter's interest." That strategy keeps you top of mind for the other person and impresses upon them that you listened and took interest in what they care about.

Familiarity—that is, more touch points—helps create a sense of affinity. When you do small, thoughtful actions for someone else, that someone else is far more likely to reciprocate down the road.

Eventually, you will establish enough of a rapport that you feel comfortable asking them for a meeting or advice.

> **Action Item**
> Identify three organizations that align with your cause of interest. Familiarize yourself with their programming and their calendars to explore events that are open to the public. Commit (to yourself) to attend at least three of their events. Meanwhile, maintain a database of people you meet, how you met them, their areas of interest, and personal details about them. The more regularly you connect with these institutions, the more opportunities you have to enhance your own credibility—and the better equipped you will be to drive change.

Simply being present in an institution or a notable situation will enhance your credibility. Over time, the goal of a citizen statesperson is to translate the credibility conferred by institutions into real and tangible impact.

Nepali-born Shilshila Acharya had long been passionate about environmental science. She began her environmental work by campaigning to plant trees along a highway in Nepal. But she wanted to do more. She started working at the Himalayan Climate Initiative, an organization leading sustainable projects in Nepal.

While she was working at the Himalayan Climate Initiative, Shilshila realized that one of the root causes of pollution in Katmandu was the overabundance of plastic bags in the city—a symbol of overconsumption and waste. With the credibility of the Himalayan Climate Initiative behind her, Shilshila was able to forge a partnership with Bhat-Bhatena, a large, well-known retail chain in Nepal. Instead of plastic, the stores began subsidizing and distributing cloth bags, helping to reduce the use of plastic bags by 33 percent. After the success of that venture, the initiative went further; it launched a campaign using the phrase "No thanks, I carry my own bag."

The campaign caught on—and eventually the government banned single-use plastics in Katmandu.

Today, Shilshila serves as the CEO of the Himalayan Climate Initiative, and she sees the campaign to ban plastic bags as an important first step in raising people's awareness about the plastic products they use. She uses her role to teach courses and plan activities to help make students throughout Nepal aware of climate change. And her ongoing partnerships have helped the initiative offer government fellowships at the local level to 60 fellows.

Resources

One of the most useful elements of established institutions is the wide array of built-in resources they offer. In some cases, those resources take the form of proprietary studies, surveys, or other informational documents and aids that can better inform you about relevant issues. Many institutions conduct their own research, or partner with other organizations to develop the deepest possible understanding of the topic they study. An affiliation to the institution can provide you with access to these works, offering a library of useful information that provides you a richer and more comprehensive feel for the subject matter.

In addition to accumulating information, institutions also collect people and professionals with experience in pertinent fields, expertise in relevant issue areas, and the ability to make an impact. Leadership figures like executive directors and CEOs are able to take actions that push the organization in productive directions. Program directors are able to connect you with exciting initiatives and groundbreaking projects. Researchers are able to answer important questions and provide useful data to inform your efforts and undergird your approach. Relationships with these individuals offer a range of benefits to grow your capacity to serve as a citizen statesperson.

Of course, established institutions don't just have access to smart and motivated personnel within the organization. They also have outside donors, supporters, and followers interested in their subject matter and enthusiastic about their work. If you as a citizen statesperson are wondering how to find supporters, a connection with an institution may offer you visibility among a significant network of external allies.

Institutions can also help you make sense of the processes that allow you to share your views and deliver thought leadership of your own. Let's say, for example, your goal is to publish and distribute an article or report that lays out useful information on your chosen topic. Some organizations will already possess a structure or financial resources to support your project. They may be affiliated with other individuals and organizations that might be interested in collaborating on a project like yours. They might even be interested in leveraging their convening power to support your vision. Without connections to these institutions and knowledge about how they operate, you might not be able to find the right levers to ensure your ideas and projects find their way into the overall conversation.

As a citizen statesperson, you serve as the ambassador for yourself and your cause. Therefore, you need to operate in several spheres.

That's why you need peers and partner organizations to leverage and take advantage of their specialization and comparative advantages. Specialists are already out there, often in the context of organizations, who will permit you to leverage their resources to fulfill your quest as a citizen statesperson. Your goal is to stay in the business of changing society. Accessing resources from established organizations can help make it happen.

Relevance

The lifeblood of an organization isn't just new funding; it's ongoing and renewed relevance. Organizations understand that if they stay static, they will wither away—losing their power, their influence, and their applicability to the world around them. Members will get older or become disengaged, and once innovative and exciting ideas will either become mainstream or fall by the wayside. That's why organizations need to be willing to learn and grow by bringing in new ideas and connecting with more people.

You want to drive change; you want to develop thought leadership; you want to promote your own branding. Effectively, you are the marketing department, the strategy department, and the manufacturer all in one. But you can't do it all yourself. As a citizen statesperson, your specialty is bringing people together and creating change. That's your highest and best use.

Of course, that won't always happen organically. New ideas arrive in waves, and from all sorts of places; we can't know whether the next big idea will come from management, the design community, technology, academia, or the front lines of grassroots activism. At the same time, organizations can't just sit back and wait for new members; they must be intentional and purposeful about searching for new opportunities to engage with the next generation of changemakers.

Here's an example. The Aspen Institute—a global nonprofit that harnesses its convening power to solve problems—consistently expands their programs to include innovators, young politicians, and policy experts. So why do they keep growing their offerings, instead of sticking to a few tried and true pressing topics? It's not because they're incapable of focusing their mission; it's because they understand that society is shifting, that technology is changing, and that the way we organize ourselves remains fluid. To connect with emerging changemakers, they need to constantly adjust their offerings, staying relevant to the topics interesting their constituents and the approaches that drive citizen statespeople around the world.

Local organizations often operate in the same way. Global:SF, for example, works to connect San Francisco to international investors and businesspeople around the world. But they also understand that to create real, long-term benefit, they need to build the architecture for continual renewal. That's why they developed a Global:SF Rising Leaders network designed to inspire innovation, support collaboration, and create new opportunities for young professionals in its communities.

These are just a few examples of programs that cater to young and emerging leaders. Many smart, effective organizations have dedicated outreach programs designed to promote continued growth and development. That hunger for renewal often provides an avenue for you—the citizen statesperson—to demonstrate your own relevance, and to gain entry to an organization.

Your Role

Here's an important point to remember: institutions aren't monoliths. They are led by a collection of people with different ideas, different approaches, and different levels of openness to change and innovation. When approaching institutions as potential partners, look for open-minded people who seem curious about learning, exploring, and asking questions about how to do things better and differently. Both of us as co-authors have worked for clients—including large companies—that might initially appear resistant to change. It's not productive to ask, "How do we get this company to change?" Instead, we ask, "Whom do I know at this company," or "Whom could I get to who would react to my questions with a thoughtful answer," or "Who might think about the question and consider a new approach?"

In a big company or a big institution, change can start at the smallest levels. Your job isn't to encourage an entire division or an entire organization to do things differently. You just need to access one person within the organization who has an internal following, and get them to take notice.

That might involve connecting with people during public conferences or social events, or even on public transportation. It might involve reaching out to them on professional social media platforms like LinkedIn with a short message that says something honest and kind about the person you are trying to meet. In many cases, we've been able to connect with executives at large companies by writing to their assistants or staffers.

You also must be prepared to speak with people as opportunities arise. In one instance, Carrie saw Michael Sneed, executive vice president, Global Corporate Affairs, and chief communications officer, at Johnson & Johnson, give a particularly insightful presentation at a conference. She perched herself outside the green room beyond the period of time that anyone else was willing to wait, and when Michael emerged, she handed him a business card with a note written on it so that he wouldn't forget who she was. But she didn't stop there; she followed up with Michael every few months for a year and a half, and sent follow-up emails documenting key takeaways from their virtual meetings so that he knew she was paying attention and that their conversations added value. Eventually, Michael agreed to participate in The Global Good Fund by serving on the board of directors.

However, it is certainly not a best practice to badger people unnecessarily, or purposely make them feel uncomfortable.

Approach people of note, find ways to talk to them, and insert yourself in a tasteful way. Remember: if you don't ask, the answer is always no.

Once you've forged contact, there are plenty of ways to engage with established organizations. You can leverage them to gain credibility by focusing on connecting with settings and people and by establishing useful relationships. You can utilize them to gain insight by accessing pertinent resources and seeking different perspectives that reflect important considerations. And you can use them to establish your relevance by sharing your insight and broader perspective, and by supporting their ongoing renewal.

Much of this work is a balancing act. Your goal is to leverage existing power structures without being constrained by the inertia that causes some of these organizations to stay tethered to the status quo. Understanding the current state of thinking on your issue is critical, but you also need to look at the world with fresh perspective and consider new approaches and applications of power that might have effective impact. Organizations may want to change, while also reticent about pushing on the leading edge of that change for fear of upsetting their existing power base. As a citizen statesperson, it's your job to navigate these challenges, and to serve as a forward-leaning force helping prod organizations into the future.

That doesn't mean you have to shackle yourself to organizations that aren't interested in change. It may be that you ultimately decide that you want to start your own organization or movement. On the other hand, you may decide that existing power bases are sufficient for what you're trying to achieve. That's up to you. The point is that some of the tools you want to leverage have already been invented—so use them. Other pieces of the puzzle need to be created—and you can do that, too. As a citizen statesperson, you are well positioned to partner with organizations to build your credibility, enhance your insight, and demonstrate your relevance as a champion for positive impact.

Discussion Questions

- What institutions in your field of interest could help you establish credibility, insight, and relevance?
- How will you connect with these institutions?
- What qualities, expertise, and information will you bring to the table to drive renewal at these institutions?

Change Starts with You

Key Takeaways

- Your success and influence as a citizen statesperson are directly related to the changes you make in your life.
- Becoming a citizen statesperson is possible no matter your age, location, experience, finances, or other perceived limitations.
- It's often possible to manage any potential risks around your citizen statesperson activities. The risks of not acting may be even greater.

MOST MAJOR ISSUES—FROM global health challenges to economic inequality to racial justice—constitute a challenge of collective action. That means the issue itself involves the aggregation of lots of people, with varied backgrounds and experiences. Fundamentally, what you're trying to achieve is change through mass practice, or a change in the way large groups of people behave.

Change starts with you. But where does it go from there? How can your actions ripple outward and translate into wider impact?

Let's begin with what you're not doing. As a changemaker and citizen statesperson, it's important that you avoid activities and actions that present a message in contrast to the one you are trying to convey. If you want to advocate for a low-carbon lifestyle, for example, don't drive a gas-powered SUV. If you're working against international child labor, don't buy clothes made in foreign sweatshops. If you're focused on water conservation, don't constantly run sprinklers, or cultivate a lush and expansive lawn.

This concept may seem simple—and it is!—but it's also incredibly important. Your personal example might not be sufficient in itself to create change, but acting in a manner contrary to the principles of your chosen issue can make it impossible for you to be heard at all.

So as you begin to step into the role of changemaker, ask yourself: am I living in the manner that I advocate? Do my actions match my ideals? Am I presenting as a good spokesperson for my cause? Getting a sense of how your actions may appear inconsistent with your words is the first step in making adjustments and decisions in your lifestyle as a citizen statesperson.

The act of changing your behavior, in fact, sends a powerful message about your commitment. Transitioning from an SUV to a low-carbon-emitting vehicle demonstrates you have skin in the game. Changing your eating habits to reduce your impact on the planet demonstrates your thoughtfulness and commitment. Just as setting a negative example can cause people to question your sincerity or push away individuals who might otherwise become connected to your cause, setting a positive example proves your bona fides and encourages like-minded individuals to take you seriously as a champion for change.

While your individual behavior might not translate into broad policy change by itself, it does set the tone for activism, and offers a standard that other people can rise to meet.

Of course, these actions aren't only for the benefit of others. By changing your habits to embody your ideals, you put your frame of mind in the right place—and that will help you develop new ideas that advance your cause.

Let's assume you've examined your own behavior to scrub it for negative examples and you've adjusted your practices to model positive attributes. That's a great start! But what comes next?

Once you are walking the walk, how do you become heard and noticed by others to grow a more expansive movement? Citizen statespeople aren't martyrs. They're not in the business of casting protest votes for the sake of protest, or setting quixotic, impossible goals. Instead, citizen statespeople are in the business of crystalizing practical solutions, and bringing new ideas into public discourse that, in time, lead to real change.

We amplify our individual examples and impacts by reaching more people, and by connecting with people who are most likely to be helpful to our cause. That's where the tools of the citizen statesperson come in handy—organizing and interacting with powerful institutions, communicating your message broadly, meeting partners that move your agenda forward, and arming yourself with ideas that strengthen your cause.

We've already discussed some of these specific tools and actions— but you should also feel free to draw upon your own unique skills and abilities to attract attention to your goals. Sami Inkinen, originally from Ruokolahti, Finland, enjoyed taking part in athletic events like Ironman competitions and triathlons. As a prediabetic, he was also passionate about healthy eating and nutrition, and wanted to garner attention to the issue of sugar consumption and its link to diabetes. Inspired by the book *Unbroken*, by Laura Hillenbrand, Sami and his wife, Meredith Loring, decided to paddle across the Pacific Ocean in a rowboat to draw attention to the cause. They became the first couple to successfully make the trip across the Pacific Ocean, rowing 2,750 miles from Monterey, California, to Hawaii and raising $200,000 to promote healthy eating. The trip also helped Sami gain attention from other leaders and advocates in the field. Sami went on to become co-founder and CEO of Virta Health, which provides the first clinically proven treatment to safely and sustainably reverse type 2 diabetes without medications or surgery.

Politics

The arena of politics presents a useful opportunity for engagement by citizen statespeople because it offers an extensive infrastructure with relatively low barriers to entry. Politicians are, by necessity, available to their constituents. To achieve their aims, policymakers must remain open to input and advocacy. Candidates for office from the local level to the federal level need all the supporters they can attract, which means they are looking to be as inclusive as possible. If you offer to extend your support and your services— and if you do so persistently and thoughtfully—then in many cases, you are able to participate in the conversation in a meaningful way.

So how does an aspiring citizen statesperson connect with a campaign or land a meeting with a policymaker? In some ways, the methods are the same ones that help you achieve connections with any other institution. Begin by looking at your network to see whether one of your close friends or contacts would be able to make an introduction to a campaign, candidate, or policymaker. Move one step beyond your personal relationships to explore whether you have appropriate contacts who are separated by one or two degrees and could plausibly make a warm introduction for you. You could leverage social media platforms like LinkedIn to explore relationships, or you could choose an issue that you care about, reach out to other people you know who care about that issue, and ask for targeted introductions.

The transparency of political organizations and institutions makes even the most impersonal approach potentially effective. You could make cold calls to campaign staff or policy offices. You could attend meetings and connect in person or digitally. Because political parties and organizations are fundamentally evangelical, they hold events open to the public at minimal or no cost, providing forums for you to create meaningful connections.

Of course, attending an event or connecting with a well-networked individual isn't the end goal, or the end of the process. You'll need to prepare for what you will do or say when you connect, and be ready to make your "elevator pitch" case. If you have a particular issue in mind, attend an event prepared to determine how your issue fits into the conversation. Find out whether the campaign, politician, or policymaker you're meeting with has an established position on the topic, or whether they are focused on issues that are connected to the issues that matter to you. Be able to draw a clear line from their priorities to your own, articulating how your issues fit into their needs.

Events and meetings are also great opportunities to explore these ideas further. You could attend an event as a fact-finding exercise. While there, ask questions to identify who is helping the candidate or policymaker explore the thought leadership issue that matters to you. If there is a person in that role, ask to get in touch to support on your shared issue. If there isn't yet a person tasked with exploring that issue, take the opportunity to explain why the issue matters. Ask the team: "Is there someone I could speak with to share why this is an important issue?" Ultimately, you might position yourself as the eventual thought leader on the topic.

Action Item

Identify a candidate or policymaker close to the issue you care about, or whom you see as a potential ally in your community. Research opportunities to get in touch, and prepare three main points explaining why your chosen issue should be of interest to them.

The key is not to think about politics as a game of winning and losing. Whether you are dealing with a policy debate or a political campaign, politics presents an opportunity to shape the concepts in the political discourse, inject new ideas into the conversation, and discover new perspectives emerging from an ongoing dialogue.

Irrespective of the outcome, if you participate in the process, participate in a campaign, you will earn valuable experience and add new skills to your citizen statesperson toolbox.

Jake Harriman is an example of a citizen statesperson who found ways to make a difference through the political and legislative process. After graduating from the United States Naval Academy, Jake served nearly eight years in the U.S. Marine Corps and led combat tours in Iraq. He saw, firsthand, what life was like for vulnerable people in unstable parts of the world. He observed how poverty and desperation could turn people towards violent extremism. And he resolved to do something about it.

After he finished his service in the military, and while he was enrolled at the Stanford Graduate School of Business, Jake founded Nuru International, an organization designed to fight terrorism by eradicating extreme poverty. But Jake also recognized that U.S. policymakers and legislators had an important role to play in supporting the principles that he was advocating. And so, for two years, Jake worked with other organizations and policymakers to help draft, introduce, and pass legislation in the U.S. Congress designed to coordinate U.S. government agencies around strategies that prevent conflict and support peacebuilding in at-risk nations. Signed into law in 2019, the Global Fragility Act that Jake helped author arms America with new tools and strategies to help reduce violence and extremism around the world.

Jake's experience working in politics and in the legislative process also made him more interested and more active in U.S. government. He became more attuned to the challenges of working within a fractured and sometimes contentious system, and more aware of the political divides that keep popular proposals from becoming law. Again, he resolved to do something—he built a new organization focused on healing those divides. As the founder and CEO of More Perfect Union, Jake is working on a 10-year plan designed to help build a viable center in U.S. politics and a movement across the country for unity and reform.

Citizen Statespersonship at Any Age

You're prepared now! You're experienced now! You're old enough (or young enough) now!

When are you prepared enough, experienced enough, or old enough to make change happen?
The answer is: now.

If you're young, great! In our fast-changing society, young people are often viewed as the best-able group to embrace or propose novel solutions, so your input is very much appreciated and desperately needed—and starting young means you have plenty of time to fulfill your potential as a citizen statesperson. If you're older, fantastic! You have gravitas and a life journey that will serve you well, offering the benefit of practical experience that is transferable to a group or a cause.

If you are inexperienced, wonderful! You may see opportunities that others miss, or be interested in exploring ideas that others have ignored or discarded. If you have a long track record in the area you're discussing, excellent! You

Like successful entrepreneurs, citizen statespeople must be willing to take risks and fail from time to time. The longer you work at being a citizen statesperson, the more resilient and effective you will become. Start now.

will be able to draw other people in, and demonstrate your knowledge and ability to drive change. Whatever life stage you are in, approach this moment as the right time to begin (or continue) your journey.

Here's an example. Autumn Adeigbo, a first-generation Nigerian-American, put in years of study and work before she could afford to launch her fashion design line. After earning a bachelor's degree at Spelman College—a historically Black women's college in Atlanta, Georgia—she studied fashion design at Parsons School of Design in New York. Autumn worked multiple jobs as she built her collection: she was a fashion assistant at W magazine, a hostess at several clubs, and a stylist for prominent designers. She started designing dresses in 2009, but didn't officially launch her brand until 2016. Her line debuted three years later.

Her approach was always values-driven. In the United States, Autumn used female-owned production facilities to uplift women across the country. In Africa, she launched four fair-trade production pilots. Known for her colorful and unique designs, Autumn embraces sustainable practices by purchasing in limited quantity, helping her to minimize fabric waste and surplus stock.

Autumn is also finding new ways to give back. She partnered with retailer Anthropologie to give a portion of the proceeds from her Spring 2021 collection sold on-site to the General Scholarship Fund at Spelman College. The funds help other young women access scholarships, academic programs, and student-faculty research opportunities, creating more chances for young women to pursue their passions.

It's been a long road for a woman who was voted "Best Dressed" in the fourth grade, but Autumn's experiences have positioned her well to create impact today and in the future.

Rejection Is Only Temporary

Not only can time mold you into a more seasoned citizen statesperson, it can also provide you with additional chances to achieve your goals.

Rejection is a familiar outcome for a citizen statesperson, because citizen statespersonship involves trying your hand at something difficult. If you're committed to becoming a citizen statesperson, it's likely that you'll face rejection far more frequently than success. That's actually a good sign that you are stretching and reaching outside your comfort zone. And rejection isn't forever. Even if you have been passed over for an interesting opportunity, the role might become available again later on—and as you've grown more experienced and more interesting yourself, you might be even more qualified to participate, and better equipped to make an impact.

Dean knows something about that. Since he was a college student, Dean was interested in joining a specific nonpartisan think tank that works to promote understanding of international relations and foreign policy. And so, years ago, Dean took a stab at applying, putting himself forward for consideration as a member of the organization that he had long respected and admired. At the time, Dean had already become somewhat known in foreign policy circles. He had taken on interesting challenges, and had a list of involvements and accomplishments. While the opportunity felt like a reach, Dean also thought he had a legitimate case to make, and that he could provide a unique and worthwhile perspective to the team.

He was turned down. But Dean—no stranger to rejection—was undeterred. He reworked his application, highlighting qualities and achievements that he thought would work to his benefit. He gained additional experience in foreign policy, adding notable achievements and roles that made him more qualified and more impactful. He lined up support from respected foreign policy experts who knew his work and his drive and who agreed to serve as enthusiastic references for his cause. And he resubmitted his candidacy, bolstered by time and expertise and made better by the organization's initial rejection.

They turned him down again. But over the years, Dean continued to be involved in the issues of foreign policy that mattered to him, finding other opportunities to contribute and make a difference. But he also kept in mind his intention to reapply to become a member of the group, undaunted by his past failures. His repeated applications weren't due to masochism or a stubborn refusal to accept defeat. He simply continued to believe that he could be a useful member of the organization if he was given the opportunity, and he wanted to keep that opportunity alive.

Finally, a couple of years ago, his application was accepted. Was it his mounting list of achievements that pushed him over the finish line? Was it the rising number of foreign-policy luminaries who attested to his worthiness and advocated for his cause? Did the right person speak out at the right time, and say exactly the right thing, to move his candidacy along? Who knows? But Dean is certainly more experienced, more accomplished, and more effective in the field than he was when he first applied all those years ago—and by accepting his candidacy now, the organization is adding a more seasoned and more well-informed individual to its ranks.

Rejection is part of the process of being a citizen statesperson, but rejection is not the end of the process. In fact, rejection can be a useful step; in the course of being denied for an opportunity, you may learn what you need to do to improve your candidacy. You may gain additional qualifications as a result, or become more thoughtful about the subject matter. If an opportunity continues to be important and relevant to you, there's simply no good reason to take it off your list.

Speaking of rejection: What if the situation is reversed? What if it's you who has turned down an opportunity to make an impact—maybe because you were worried you weren't ready, or you thought you weren't qualified to participate? Have you missed your chance?

Maybe not! In fact, this might be the perfect time to reconnect and reengage with opportunities gone by.

Four years ago, a woman named Lily Yeh asked Carrie to help manage the business she founded called Little Loving Hands. She and Carrie had met through The Global Good Fund, where Lily was a fellow while Carrie was CEO. Lily created an impactful business to teach kids kindness through crafting, but she didn't enjoy operating the company as much as she enjoyed product design. At the time Lily reached out, Carrie was pregnant with her second child and was neck-deep into growing The Global Good Fund. Carrie didn't think the timing was right to add another business to the mix, so she politely turned down the opportunity, and eventually the lack of a partner caused Lily to shut down the business.

Two years later, Carrie was speaking at a 500-person event for women professionals. Upon learning that Carrie was the mother of young children, several audience members asked, "How do you teach kids kindness?" It's a fair question; after all, The Global Good Fund exists to create more social good in the world by growing high-potential young leaders. But Carrie's response was, "I know as much as you do about how to grow kindness in kids."

She immediately thought of Little Loving Hands, and the inquiries prompted her to reach out to Lily to restart her company. They enlisted the help of another outstanding business partner, Jen Pollard, to manage all aspects of business operation. And together they rebuilt Little Loving Hands into a company that provides kids with boxes of craft kits that focus on teaching kids kindness. Today, both Carrie and Jen take their children to help work on the business behind the scenes, and to events where they can connect with other children and adults who care about creating a kinder world.

Don't talk yourself out a good opportunity. And don't completely rule out opportunities you previously passed on. Whether you're new to the citizen statespersonship role, or finding new ways to give back after decades of service, you are needed—and needed now.

Your Job Is Not You

It is tempting to define ourselves by one job or role that occupies the bulk of our time or what we do. In part, that's a reflection of the world we live in. We have a natural tendency to typecast others—not out of any sort of malice or with any nefarious intent, but because it's quick and simple to categorize people, particularly by their professions. Whether you're a waiter or an accountant or a lion tamer—and especially, perhaps, if you're a lion tamer—your job or your main activity provides an easy shorthand to others to remember who you are.

The trouble is that when we internalize those archetypes, we can find ourselves tethered to them—and then if the role ends, or the opportunity vanishes, we can become adrift, unable to articulate who we are, what we do, or why we matter. Without that anchor, a person's mental health can suffer.

That's a real concern—and one we have seen firsthand. We have seen an aspiring athlete dedicate his entire existence to major league baseball before suddenly sustaining a career-ending injury. We have seen a political staffer and policy advisor methodically follow a set career path, only to watch his next job disintegrate in the wake of a disappointing election season. If you define yourself based on one linear set of accomplishments, and then your world spins off its axis, it can be difficult to find your bearings and deeply challenging to your sense of self-worth.

As a citizen statesperson, you need to embrace a different attitude.

Focus on the skills you develop, rather than the jobs you hold.

This is important, because jobs can be temporary and limiting, while skills are lasting and transferable. That's true even of jobs you didn't enjoy, or jobs that you saw as temporary stopovers on a larger, longer career.

Did your time in the service industry teach you how to relate to customers? Excellent! That'll help you connect with investors and sponsors. Did your role in finance teach you to read a balance sheet? Great! That'll come in handy in the nonprofit space. Did your experience as a lion tamer teach you to be brave? Good! You'll be a hit in board meetings.

With every role or responsibility you take on—either in your professional career, or in your personal life—ask yourself, what are you learning now? What do you know now that you didn't know a year ago? What can you do now that you couldn't do before? Every new skill you hone or acquire supplements the tools in your toolbelt. Unlike a particular job or role, those skills will stay with you over time, providing you with a reservoir of competencies and capabilities that you can apply to any relevant opportunity. Investing in yourself and building up your skill set will make you feel more fulfilled while also giving you more opportunities to make an impact.

Second, plan to do lots of things at once. It's useful diversification to place plenty of rods in the fire. You may not know which rod is going to ignite or when, but by pursuing a range of projects and opportunities, you avoid tying all your hopes and dreams to one outcome and you improve your ultimate odds of success. At the same time, pursuing a range of projects and opportunities means that any one rejection will have only a minor impact on your sense of self. That way, although rejection may be disappointing, it is not defining.

To some people, having plenty of rods in the fire may sound unfocused, but for a citizen statesperson it's key to staying connected with yourself and with others. That's true even at the highest levels. Carrie, for example, has a full-time job at The Global Good Fund, she's simultaneously the managing director at Global Impact Fund II, an investment fund that she's seeking to grow significantly, and a "hobby company" in Little Loving Hands. She also serves on corporate and nonprofit boards, does public speaking, volunteers in her local community, and is a wife and also a mother to three young children—all while co-authoring this book. No single role defines her completely; instead, each role contributes to the others as well as Carrie's sense of self. These roles combine to help her create social impact.

Occasionally, Carrie will hear from people who ask how she has the bandwidth to take on so many projects. To Carrie, it's the coalescence of roles and activities that makes her effective. She decided a long time ago that she didn't want her legacy or her identity to be governed by any one project. Instead, she was intentional about her approach, and committed to building a portfolio that makes change at scale. She also aligned herself with a support system that understands her approach.

That brings us to a third important point: enlist others to serve as advisors and mentors. Being a citizen statesperson doesn't mean being a one-person show. You can, and must, bring others along if you want to go the distance.

It's not always easy to recognize your own value, or to see how your skills align with potentially interesting opportunities. An outside perspective—especially from someone who understands and appreciates your worth—will help you identify optimal places to apply your talents. By bringing in mentors from different sectors and industries, and with different focuses and personalities, you gain broader perspective and access more diverse opportunities.

Assembling a team of advisors also serves another purpose. When you face challenges and failures, it's easy to feel alone. One of the supports that keeps us going when times are tough is having a strong group of friends, mentors, and professional colleagues that we like and respect. They have imparted great advice and support over the years, and validated our efforts during difficult times. Perhaps most importantly, they encourage us to do the work we care about, and motivate us to apply our skills in the service of our mission.

So how does all of this work together? Let us illustrate in this way: for years, people in Dean's orbit have referred to his collection of political and civic activities, philanthropic projects, business ventures, and personal networks as "Dean, Inc."—a multidisciplinary endeavor that pulls together a variety of different ideas, undertakings, and people under one broad mission.

Think of yourself as Your Name, Inc.: a scrappy company or organization with a diverse portfolio. What is your overarching company mission? Who is on your board of advisors? What are the various goals and objectives you are trying to achieve in the service of your mission? What comparative advantages do you hold, and what tools and skills do you have at your disposal? What opportunities do you have for expansion or special projects? By taking this approach, you can build an identity that takes into account your full scope of interests and abilities—giving you a more stable base permitting you to reach for different opportunities and pivot throughout your career, without losing your sense of identity or your self-esteem.

It won't always be easy. Actually, it'll hardly ever be easy. You'll face challenges, some of them significant. But if you focus on your skills, broaden your scope, and connect with others, you'll be prepared, supported, and able to partake in causes that make you happy and make an impact at the same time.

Location, Location, Location

We've already discussed how the right setting can help you make a stronger impact. Creating a backdrop of authority and professionalism by meeting in a location that is relevant to your issue area—or to thought leadership in general—helps you to be taken seriously as a citizen statesperson.

Let's take a step back and consider the role of location in general. What part does your physical location play in your journey towards citizen statespersonship?

Certainly, physical location in an area housing institutions of leadership around your issue area can be extremely helpful. If you're interested in humanitarian aid and refugee support, living near the International Rescue Committee headquarters in New York City might provide relevant opportunities to make connections and have interactions that are unavailable to people who live elsewhere. If you're focused on ending poverty, being near the U.S. headquarters of an organization like CARE in Atlanta may prove useful. Many philanthropic organizations and NGOs have headquarters in Washington, D.C., offering a central location for meetings and contacts. Be aware of the relevant people and organizations in your area so that you make the appropriate connections.

Still, not every citizen statesperson is located in close geographic proximity to a thought leader or institution germane to their cause. If you are one of the many, many people who live in a different part of the country or world from the people with whom you seek to network, don't fret! There are terrific opportunities for virtual networking that provide a similar level of interaction—to seek those opportunities. If you cannot attend an event in person, participate digitally if that's an option. Follow up with the speakers or attendees you sought to network with at the event, acknowledging a detail, an event experience, or a moment of the conference that you found particularly resonant. Connect your experience with their leadership, and make yourself part of the conversation. Especially in the wake of the COVID-19 pandemic, virtual networking has become the norm, making it more acceptable and effective to connect with fellow citizen statespeople over the Internet, no matter where in the country or world you live.

Remember that learning and leadership don't only happen within our own communities. In-person travel, when possible, can provide useful insights. In some cases, that might mean traveling to institutions of scholarship or authority on a subject that interests you. In other cases, it might mean exploring far-off communities deeply connected to the issue you are studying in order to glean on-the-ground information. The very best solutions you bring to bear on an issue should draw on the widest array of data, and many of the social, political, and economic challenges of our time exist far beyond any ocean or border. Globalized issues require varied viewpoints, and we can learn from the experiences of other groups and populations. Where possible, travel gives the citizen statesperson a window into how other people grapple with similar problems—and may offer useful insights and solutions.

These opportunities may turn on your ability to self-fund as well. You may be able to obtain travel funding from community organizations and support systems that work in the areas you care about, or connect with national groups that support learning opportunities around the world. In fact, plenty of think tanks, nonprofits, and advocacy organizations offer financial resources to individuals who seek to undertake work with a purpose. Dean and Carrie met and eventually went on to become co-authors as a result of leveraging these opportunities! A few organizations that offer financial support and personal development are listed in the appendix at the end of this book.

The point is that geographic location can provide opportunities to learn and grow as a citizen statesperson—location can also create challenging barriers, but your location does not prevent you from finding success as a citizen statesperson.

Managing Risk

It may be daunting to realize that you need to step up on a particular issue. You may wonder why someone else hasn't stepped up before. You may worry about the risks of "putting yourself out there" as a citizen statesperson.

We're not going to dismiss the potential implications. Those risks and challenges are real. You could encounter risks to your reputation as you make yourself more visible to those who disagree with your viewpoints. You could find yourself taking financial risks by investing in yourself through travel opportunities, organization memberships, or other opportunities for access and development. You might encounter social risks as you become more vocal about issues that matter to you and potentially find yourself in conflict with friends, family members, or individuals in your community.

These are real concerns, but they need not prevent you from engaging on issues you care about, nor prevent you from taking action to effect much-needed change. Instead, take steps to minimize risks while recognizing the value of your work. To reduce risks to your reputation, for example, be thoughtful about the way you speak, write, and act in public forums, ensuring that you are taking a measured and reasonable tone and maintaining a respectful and reasonable attitude. To alleviate the impacts on your finances, track a careful budget that provides you with funds for travel, if possible, and other development opportunities without stretching yourself too thin. Engage in outreach to organizations and programs that can help fund your work.

When it comes to the intersection of your social circles and your causes, you have three basic options. You can try to convert your personal friends to your causes, and use that experience as a test of your abilities to shape minds and actions. You can decide to leave your work at the door when you speak with personal friends or connections whose viewpoints may not align with your efforts to keep the peace. Or you may find that the trade-off is reasonable, and that you prefer weeding out certain social contacts who disagree with your strongly held views and instead make new close contacts through your work who share your interests.

These are all valid approaches to mitigate potential risks of citizen statespersonship, and you may find additional ways to make your approach easier and more effective. While these thoughts are natural and necessary (Taking a stand is daunting! You will face obstacles and setbacks!) you mustn't let them consume your work or dissuade you from achieving your potential. Remember to weigh the risks of inaction as well, and the implications for the ideas and causes you care about if you don't do your part.

That's something Dean experiences often, even today. As a lawyer in private practice, he needs to be trusted by clients on a range of issues, and expressing strong views outside of his professional role might alienate individuals and organizations that would otherwise seek him out. As Dean says, lawyers are not just nonpartisan; they sometimes need to take a stand as a vote of confidence in the process itself. Being active in citizen statespersonship can create obstacles to that goal.

In one instance, a colleague reached out to warn Dean that he might undermine his professional brand through his work to engage with individuals and leaders from across the political spectrum. Dean had been writing articles on leadership in national publications, hosting spirited public forums with prominent experts from the conservative and liberal movements, and creating opportunities for sometimes-controversial leaders to share their views. To Dean's colleague, Dean's activities constituted an unnecessary and potentially costly risk, and he urged Dean to dial it back.

Dean saw the calculation differently. He viewed his work as an opportunity to push conversations forward, and to help foster understanding between people who wouldn't otherwise find themselves in a room together. It was certainly possible that some onlookers would see the prominent people he had hosted and associate Dean with that person's views—but to Dean, avoiding that kind of association was less important than gaining an understanding of what people were thinking in order to find common ground.

Carrie has experienced similar pressures in her experience at The Global Good Fund. In one instance, she invited a well-known conservative woman who had been a business leader and a presidential candidate to speak to the organization. In the days after the invitation became public, Carrie received a raft of emails from social entrepreneurs who were furious with the choice, who disagreed with the speaker's views and advocacy, and who threatened to boycott the meeting.

That could have caused Carrie to back down, and to pull the speaker from the agenda. She could have decided that a provocative participant would create too much controversy for the organization, and that the selection would call into question her own fitness as a leader of the project and a representative of her cause. For Carrie, though, there was value in the disagreement—and when she responded to irate emails or angry calls, she explained that she was simply inviting social entrepreneurs to hear a different perspective on leadership. As Carrie saw it, her job was to facilitate a dialogue, and to move the conversation forward by bringing together parties and groups that might not have interacted in the first place.

In both our cases, acting like a citizen statesperson came with a certain amount of risk. We were able to manage that risk to an extent—in part by making sure we were serving as facilitators of a conversation rather than activists pushing a particular viewpoint. But at the end of the day, we were also committed to our goal and determined to create a dialogue, even if that dialogue might involve (or generate) tension.

It's worth keeping in mind that, while you can reduce the risk you may incur as a citizen statesperson, you can never totally eliminate it. You will occasionally find yourself encountering opposition or pushback—even frustration and derision. You can't control how other people react to your actions. If you are confident in your goals, though, you can weather any criticism, and keep your eyes on our obligation as citizen statespeople to create discourse and drive impact.

Standing your ground won't be easy! Remind yourself that your work is important, that the payoff is worth the risk, and that it's up to you to make the kind of change you believe in. After all, ideas don't independently navigate the neural networks of human persuasion and human society all by themselves. Ideas are silent thoughts or words on paper—right until the moment that an individual steps up to turn them into reality.

Every idea needs a human promoter. Every cause requires people to lead. Social change requires people to drive it forward. You have an opportunity, now and always, to do your part.

Discussion Questions

- What behavior will you model to demonstrate your commitment to your values and your cause? What changes will you make personally, or in your professional life to demonstrate that commitment?
- How does your geographic location impact your ability to serve as a citizen statesperson? How does your location make your work harder? What opportunities does your location provide?
- What are the risks you might personally face on your journey as a citizen statesperson? How will you mitigate or manage those risks?

What Does It Take to Be a Citizen Statesperson?

Key Takeaways

- Storytelling is central to the success of a citizen statesperson.
- Self-reflection is important for determining your limits, when to be flexible, and whom to rely on to complement your efforts.
- As a citizen statesperson, you are always representing others, and they may be from competing stakeholder groups.

THERE IS A wide range of strengths, qualities, and tools that a person can bring to bear to solve social problems or make an impact in one's community, but the most fundamental skills are often the most powerful ones. Just as successful athletes continue to practice the fundamentals of their sport, successful citizen statespeople continue to hone the fundamental skills that help them improve, grow, and thrive.

So what are the fundamental skills of a citizen statesperson? What are the tools to hone, sharpen, and revitalize? In our view, there are at least seven skills that every citizen statesperson must learn, practice, and sharpen over time: storytelling, empathy, representation, perspective, self-reflection, flexibility, and teamwork.

Storytelling

That's no small task. Different people possess a variety of interests and backgrounds. They are motivated by a range of factors, arguments, and experiences. To connect with others and build a committed constituency for your issues and goals, you will need to tell your story effectively, and frame your story in a way that is relevant, relatable, and compelling for your audience.

So how do you do it?

For the citizen statesperson, a good story has three parts: it informs people by sharing your knowledge of the subject with your audience and

Citizen statespersonship requires you to articulate a vision and connect with people both emotionally and analytically. You need to be able to explain why your vision has merit, why your proposals make sense, and why other people should invest in your work and your approach.

by enhancing your audience's understanding of the subject matter. Your story persuades people by convincing them of your point of view and by generating consensus and agreement around your issue or idea. Your story motivates people to take action, encouraging your audience to share your passion and to take specific steps that create meaningful impact.

While the core message and core values you offer remain constant, tweak your story to speak in a targeted way to different audiences. Before you address specific groups or individuals, take a moment to understand who they are. Who are you trying to motivate? Is it a small

Your universal story is most effective when it frames the challenge you're addressing and places you and the audience in the context of that story— ideally both as impacted individuals and as change agents who are part of the solution.

community, or a wide swath of people? How do they connect with your area of interest and your overall mission? What are their goals, and how does your chosen issue impact them? Use that knowledge to tailor your approach in ways that help the audience see themselves in the story.

Of course, storytelling isn't just about the people you're speaking to; it's also about the way you tell stories. Dean experienced this principle during an interview with a candidate seeking a fellowship. The man was explaining to a review committee the value of the tool he was developing—a hand-held device that could be used to provide medical imaging to remote communities. Using semiconductors, artificial intelligence, and cloud technology, the device could offer whole-body medical images to people around the world for a relatively low cost.

Sounds great, right? Except . . . it didn't sound great in the room. The man was having trouble communicating with the group, connecting with the audience, and explaining the purpose or importance of his device. The review team was having a hard time understanding how the device worked, or the value it provided. And about 45 minutes into the hour-long interview, it was clear the conversation wasn't going well.

Finally, Dean asked, "Do you happen to have the device with you?"

"Oh," said the man. "Yeah."

And he pulled out the device.

It was as if everything had changed. A switch had been flipped, and the uncomfortable, unsure man was suddenly in his element, explaining the product, detailing its applications, and making a compelling case for its use. The committee was mesmerized.

The point is, there's more than one way to tell a story, and more than one way to reach an audience. A picture may be worth a thousand words; an in-person meeting might convey more richness and texture than a phone call; an experience might be more dynamic and revealing than a conversation; a delivery that animates you is likely to be more effective than one that doesn't tap into your own excitement.

As you consider how to communicate your story, look inward first; think about what initially drew you to the idea or cause.

What was the powerful experience that sparked your interest? What made you envision the path forward? How will you reach people in a similarly inspiring way? Extrapolate your experience to the world that you're trying to move, consider how to convey the fullest sense of what you're trying to accomplish, and include the elements that will help you do exactly that.

Empathy

That requires the capability to envision yourself through the prism of other people's reality, and to recognize and identify with the lived experiences of individuals around you.

As a citizen statesperson, you are a representative of your cause. To be a successful representative, you must be able to connect with people from every part of society.

In practice, the application of empathy can involve a series of questions. Before you begin a conversation, ask yourself: What cause or what organization am I representing? What core values drive that cause or organization? How will I try to advance the cause? Think about the needs of the stakeholders you're addressing. Why should the person I'm engaging with find my cause compelling? How does their experience align with my experience? Where do our experiences differ? How do I see myself and my cause in their personal or organizational mission? And, crucially, how would I feel about these perspectives if I were the person on the other end of the dialogue? That kind of thoughtfulness should be applied to every interaction.

Demonstrating empathy isn't always easy or natural. You may find yourself in a range of settings, from the slums to the boardroom, dealing with a range of people, from activists and fellow travelers to opposing interest groups and concerned individuals. You may encounter people you disagree with or dislike, but who are nonetheless important to your mission. That's why it's so important to practice empathy, to refine your ability to recognize the challenges and struggles other people face, and to find ways to relate to others with compassion and understanding.

Empathy is also critical when it comes to interactions across borders and communities. The narratives, stories, and morals that resonate with one society could mean something very different in a different cultural context. If you're not empathetic, you may hit discordant notes that either drown out or undermine your message and your mission. When you are empathetic, the harmony of your communications will ensure your interactions are as compelling as possible.

Here's an example. Years ago, Dean was speaking at an international conference in Seoul, South Korea, to diplomatic and government representatives from more than 40 countries, and the topic of American Exceptionalism came up.

American Exceptionalism is the idea that the United States is inherently different from other nations, that the country's values and history are unique and worthy of universal admiration. Is that a useful argument for an American to make in a room filled with people from around the world proudly representing their own nations? Probably not!

Dean understood that touting American Exceptionalism in this context and moment would be a problematic move for a representative of the United States, so he shifted the conversation in a more inclusive direction. He asked the group to consider how far their own countries had come in terms of building democratic resilience and the rule of law, and what that progress meant to them. Instead of underscoring a narrower narrative, he tried to appeal to universal values.

Diplomacy is at the core of citizen statespersonship, and a central tenet of diplomacy is that commonalities and strategic interests outweigh differences when collaborating across borders and boundaries. That's why citizen statespeople must continually ask themselves: How will what I say be interpreted? Is there a more universalized way to deliver my message? How can I ensure that my story is resonating with the broadest possible audience?

Here's the bottom line: every individual is the protagonist of their own story. If you are seen as dismissive of a person's experience or viewpoint, you will alienate potential allies and critical partners. If you ignore a person's background or cultural influences, you may come across as shallow and small-minded. By approaching other people with the recognition that their concerns and experiences are of paramount importance to them, and uncovering core connections that bring you together, you will create shared bonds that make your work more impactful.

Representation

A citizen statesperson is more than just one individual; a citizen statesperson is a representative of a cause, an idea, and a movement.

That means that a citizen statesperson bears a responsibility to serve as an effective spokesperson and a goodwill ambassador, which requires avoiding activities or behaviors that draw undue or untoward scrutiny or criticism. Conversely, it means taking part in activities or behaviors that draw positive attention or improve the reputation of the group. And it means being able to speak from a broader point of view than just one's own.

That last point is crucial, and more challenging than it seems. If you don't accurately capture the viewpoints of the constituents you represent, you may say things that are inconsistent with your cause or mission.

That's a challenge Carrie experienced firsthand. In 2014, Carrie was invited by a Global Good Fund Ambassador to help facilitate a workshop in Bosnia alongside an enterprise called Mozaik, which provides grants and advisory and leadership development support for rural initiatives to aid social and economic development in Bosnia and Herzegovina. She laid out a workshop schedule the same way she had previously for partners in the United States and other parts of the world: with a presentation immediately followed by a hands-on learning activity designed to engage the audience in practical application. Yet when she was ready to move on to the active portion of the workshop, the ambassador paused the presentation, and suggested they stick with the listening portion for the first day and come back to a more active session the following day, when they'd had a chance to digest and reflect on what they had heard. According to the ambassador, splitting those two portions of the event was a more traditional way to approach the process, grounded in a cultural foundation that had its roots in recent Bosnian history.

For Carrie, it was an eye-opening experience to discover how culture and history could impact the way a team approached a workshop. She saw it as an example of how studying a culture could help individuals be more in tune with their audience. When Carrie returned to the United States, she wrote about her experience and what she learned. She discussed factors that she understood to be at the heart of the cultural distinction and praised the people she had met, highlighting their focus on thoughtful understanding and reflection rather than blind or dogmatic action.

After the article was published, Carrie received a call from the ambassador she had worked with on her trip. Some of the participants in the workshop had read her article—and they weren't happy. While she had intended to praise their approach to learning and engagement, they had viewed her depiction as condescending and hurtful. They weren't asking her to take down the article, but they did want her to understand that it had caused hurt feelings among the group.

Carrie was mortified. She had written the article to provide a platform to an important organization and highlight a group of talented individuals, and instead, she had offended them. She apologized to the team, and she worked to learn from what happened. Today, when writing about her experiences, Carrie not only reads her work carefully to consider whether it might cause offense, she also shares every article in advance with the people the article describes to ensure her words won't be misconstrued or misunderstood.

Here's the point: representation is challenging. It can be difficult to sync perfectly with a group to which you don't personally belong. Even if you arrive with the best of intentions, you may not foresee every outcome or anticipate every speed bump or roadblock. Rather than assuming you have all the answers, make sure you check in with people more connected to the community than you are; ask them for a gut check as you form your own opinions, and be especially thoughtful about the lived experiences of the people with whom you work.

Challenges like this one also show why it's so critical to forge positive relationships and to be respectful about your interactions. In Carrie's case, her words accidentally upset a key constituency, but they didn't upend the relationship. The people involved knew who she was, recognized her positive motivations, and understood that it was an issue of inartful expression and not malicious intent. Should you work to avoid inartful expressions? Absolutely! But if you do occasionally make missteps, a foundation of goodwill will help you weather the fallout.

Still, representation is about more than avoiding embarrassment, or even building a positive reputation for your organization or cohort.

Imagine a parent telling a college-bound child, "You represent our family in every decision you make." On one level, that statement can be construed as a threat (and sometimes, it's intended precisely that way)—putting the burden on the individual to constrain their own behavior and limit their activity to prevent negative outcomes. That message can also be empowering, because it reminds the individual that they are not a sole actor; that they come from a community, and can draw strength from the family they represent.

In the same way, citizen statespeople must represent their communities effectively to mitigate harm, while also recognizing that the community they represent offers them additional authority and support. Practicing your ability to serve as an effective representative of your mission, organization, or field can help you project confidence, gather additional assistance, and demonstrate your own value as a leader while forging closer ties with the people you are seeking to lead.

In Carrie's work with The Global Good Fund, she interacts with a range of communities and organizations, and encounters all sorts of attitudes and preformed opinions about nonprofits, nonprofit leaders, and people of her own background. What she has found in her experience is that sitting down and having intimate one-on-one or small-group conversations can be an effective way to communicate that her intentions are genuine, that her approach is effective, and that she cares about connecting productively. In fact, she expands this strategy to other individuals on her team, working to expose them frequently to donors, partners, and served communities in small group settings so that all parties get to know each other. This strategy helps to engender trust, forge positive relationships, and improve representation of her organization and of the people she serves.

The most important lesson to remember is that, as a citizen statesperson, you are constantly acting as an ambassador for your organization and your cause. That means you need to be intentional about the way you communicate—in your words, in your writing, and even in the way you dress and present yourself. Whether you are visiting entrepreneurs, interacting with donors, or meeting with impacted communities, be reflective of the local environment and culture. That's a positive way to be an ambassador for a cause and a steward for change.

Perspective

One key signifier of a citizen statesperson is the ability to scale leadership to recognize how solutions can be expanded or fit to larger or more expansive challenges. After all, not every leader is a citizen statesperson. A traditional leader might have an influential role in his or her neighborhood or professional community. As a citizen statesperson, though, you need to be willing and able to take your cause beyond borders, to speak on behalf of a broader group, and to scale your actions to encompass more universal themes, shared identities, and cooperative endeavors. That requires a clear sense of perspective.

Let's consider an example. A Parent Teacher Association member may be a respected leader in her community—but that doesn't automatically make her a citizen statesperson. The change occurs when she decides that her experience and her viewpoint should be shared as part of a greater dialogue. What if she connects with a group of visiting educators from abroad, or joins an organization that unites educators from different walks of life? Now she's putting her experience and leadership into a broader context by elevating her leadership for greater impact.

That's citizen statespersonship. This PTA member may bring the lessons she learns back to her community, or she may help broader groups come up with new and improved best practices.

To be effective as a citizen statesperson, approach your journey as an opportunity to grow your impact—that means understanding where you are, and where you want to go.

By elevating her activity and her leadership, she's also elevating the dialogue, her own community, and a larger group at the same time. That's what distinguishes her as a citizen statesperson: the ability to lift her leadership to a higher plane.

Are there ways you can bring your skills or passions to a more expansive audience? Can you use your connections, resources, and current leadership roles to magnify your work? How can you take what you've already learned and apply it in a larger way?

Doniece Sandoval was a marketing executive who raised her family in a trendy San Francisco neighborhood. But as housing prices soared, she saw elderly residents evicted from their homes and turned out onto the street. As the homeless population swelled, Doniece looked for ways to provide assistance in a scalable manner.

One day, Doniece heard a homeless woman on the street shouting, "I will never be clean!" This plea for basic hygiene facilities moved Doniece to explore what kinds of options were available for the city's homeless population—and she discovered that there were only 16 shower facilities for thousands of homeless people in San Francisco.

Doniece got to work. The city was in the midst of replacing its old public buses, and Doniece crowdfunded to raise $75,000 to secure and retrofit the buses with showers and toilets. Since the buses couldn't carry large water tanks, she received permission for them to tap fire hydrants and heat water on-site.

In the course of one year, Doniece launched Lava Mae, a nonprofit designed to bring mobile showers to people moving through homelessness. Since 2013, the organization has expanded to serve more than 32,000 Californians with their mobile hygiene units, providing more than 78,000 showers to populations in San Francisco, Los Angeles, and Venice.

The organization has also broadened the scope of its care. It pioneered Pop-Up Care Villages that bring together public agencies, nonprofits, and social entrepreneurs to provide dental and health support, and help people register for California's

Medicaid healthcare program. People experiencing homelessness can also receive haircuts, clothing, and job counseling at these temporary sites. During the COVID-19 pandemic, Lava Mae pivoted to create a program around handwashing stations and developed a hygiene kit for people in need.

Since Lava Mae launched, other locations around the world have created approaches to serve the people experiencing homelessness that were inspired by Lava Mae's model. To date, the organization that Doniece built in her backyard has supported over 250 groups working in 200 communities around the world.

Doniece could have used her resources to create a smaller local impact. She could have given funds to individuals or supported a more limited neighborhood response. But she saw the opportunity and recognized her own ability to expand her work, to broaden her efforts, and to build a program and a network that could change lives in an expansive and replicable way.

That's what citizen statesperson perspective looks like.

Self-Reflection

Citizen statespersonship isn't just about looking outward. It's also about a sense of self. You need to feel comfortable in your own skin, clear on your core values, and confident about your own vision for change. If citizen statespersonship is capable of super-empowering the individual for our modern age, it's important that the individual understands exactly who they are and what they are trying to achieve. Once you firmly grasp your own core values, you can begin to recognize how they play out against other people's interests and needs.

What are you good at? What do you struggle with? What are the ideas and issues that excite you and move you to action? What ways could you improve? In which fundamental areas of expertise do you need more practice or assistance? What have you achieved—and what action is still to come?

Understanding the answers to these questions is key to citizen statespersonship because they help you sharpen your problem-solving skills, your self-awareness and sense of agency, and even your own sense of civic responsibility. It's not enough to move blindly in one direction; a citizen statesperson needs to question his or her methods, examine his or her progress, and constantly consider ways to improve performance.

We often learn by experiences and mistakes, but unless we take time to question ourselves about what experiences mean and think actively about them, it's unlikely that we will embark upon significant changes. Self-reflection is a process that helps us move from experience to understanding—encouraging self-awareness, helping to identify areas of improvement, and allowing us to recognize what works and what doesn't. It also presents us with an opportunity to reflect more deeply about how effectively we achieve our goals, and what we might do to improve our processes and ourselves.

That opportunity is key. The world is a chaotic place, and the life of a citizen-statesperson is often fast-moving and frenzied. It may leave precious little time for deep thought and consideration. That's why it's imperative to make the time to deliberately consider yourself and your approach, and to think about any needed changes. Are you working with the partners you want? Are you taking the action you want? Are you representing your cause and your community effectively, in a way that promotes sustained and durable change?

Self-reflection is hard—and it tends to get harder. The further along you move in your career path and leadership journey, the more set in your ways you tend to become, and the greater the effort needed to adjust your behavior and approach. That's why it's so important to get in the habit of self-reflection early, to dedicate time to the practice, and to develop your self-reflection muscle.

Here's an action item:

Write your thoughts in a journal and chart progress. Make this time a standing appointment, so you continue the habit of self-reflection.

Identify one day per week when you will spend 30 minutes in active self-reflection. Use that time to consider how you are living up to your potential as a citizen statesperson, and what adjustments are needed to be more effective.

Flexibility

Uncertainty and ambiguity are the new normal. Today's economic, social, and political institutions and practices are in a constant state of flux. As a citizen statesperson, you must navigate that changing landscape; that will require you to become comfortable with change.

In part, navigating a changing landscape requires revisiting your assumptions and ideas. Stay engaged in the latest thinking about your chosen issue, and examine new research and information that might affect the way you think about the topic. No individual has all the answers, and it's important to be open to persuasion and ready to consider new developments as you adjust your views. As you learn, you discover more effective approaches and new opportunities to drive impact.

Years ago, for example, meat producers and processors might have dismissed vegetarian tastes as exotic. Today, shifting practices and new technology have made vegetarian meat companies like the Jackfruit Company, Beyond, and Impossible enormous success stories that deliver a whole new line of products to an expanding market. That's the story of how some of the world's largest meat producers became meat alternative producers as well. If you were a citizen statesperson focused on reducing meat consumption, the emergence of alternative meat products might change your ideas about what is possible and how best to approach your chosen goal. Being open to that kind of change is critical.

Along with intellectual and creative flexibility, citizen statespeople need to be flexible in their partnerships. Not every alliance will be a perfect fit, and not every collaborator will operate in the same way you operate. Leaders come from all walks of life, and the people who may seem to be at odds now may later become your strongest supporters. As Voltaire said, "Don't let the perfect be the enemy of the good," and don't dismiss someone's ability to help just because they don't share your background or your specific approach. One of the most important tools in a citizen statesperson's toolbox is the ability to bring together disparate interests and stakeholders to drive impact—doing so requires you to be flexible in the partners and allies you select.

This is a useful approach defensively, because the more connections you make, the fewer people are motivated to derail you—but you may also find that investing time and energy to connect with people who might be

As a general rule, it's useful to maintain positive relationships with people, whether you see them as competitors or close confidants. Put effort into the people who support you. Put effort into people who are your detractors.

inclined to be your detractors can actually help unearth hidden allies and points of agreement. In fact, if you're willing to invest even minimal energy in unlikely places with a constructive approach and attitude, you may find that your investments pay off with long-term potential moonshot rewards.

So how do you decide when to be flexible, and when to hold your ground? Here's an important cautionary note: maintaining flexibility in ideas, methods, and partnerships does not require losing sight of your core values. That's where the other fundamentals—like self-reflection and perspective—play important roles. Whether you are considering altering your approach to your position, or your methods, or your partnerships, the citizen statesperson makes a judgment call on a situational basis. For example, if one of your core values is to support freedom of the press, how do you feel about working with a more restrictive government? If you do decide to engage, you need to continue evaluating the situation on an ongoing basis. Are your partners evolving and improving as you continue to collaborate, or are you contributing to a halo on a bad actor?

Staying in touch with your core values and core goals will help you decide when to make adjustments, and when to part ways with a partner or approach.

Teamwork

Look, even we sometimes get surprised at how far people can go—and how much they can achieve—with glaring gaps in their fundamental leadership skills.

There are a couple of ways to think about that phenomenon. One possibility is that it demonstrates that fundamentals don't really matter as much as we might believe, and that these proficiencies are overrated. Another option is that the overall makeup of leadership is so broad and encompasses so many dimensions that it's unrealistic to expect one person to embody all these traits, and that a healthy mixture of these attributes can get you most of the way to your goal. A third possibility is that these deficiencies are, in fact, taking a toll—and that these individuals could be significantly more successful if they were willing to go back and work on their leadership fundamentals.

What if you are a person with one of these gaps? Yes, you should work on your fundamentals. Yes, you should lean into areas where you feel you are strongest. But you can also create partnerships with individuals, colleagues, and organizations to help fill these gaps. Part of your role as a citizen statesperson is to connect organizations and stakeholders to generate a greater impact—so why not use those skills to connect yourself to others with fundamental skills and proficiencies that complement your own?

Do you struggle with perspective? Connect with someone who's great at scaling leadership! Are you sometimes inflexible? Link up with someone who helps you see other approaches and opportunities you might otherwise miss! Do you feel unrepresentative of the community you are trying to support? Make common cause with an individual or organization more closely connected to the population in question! These are all ways to use teamwork to strengthen your work as a citizen statesperson and to create the best possible results.

Let us be clear: these fundamental skills do not guarantee success. Citizen statespersonship is a challenging vocation, and there are plenty of obstacles that can trip you up along the way. But by honing these proficiencies, you can build a foundation for success. If you don't already have these fundamental leadership skills, find or create ways to build them. If you feel confident about your skills, find ways to advance them further. Read books about self-improvement and seek out workshops and seminars that help you develop these attributes. Examine history, read memoirs from leaders you admire, or go online to watch videos of the ways leaders convey ideas and relate to other people.

Two lessons are vital to bear in mind. First, lack of fundamental skill in one area is no reason to give up. Don't listen to the inner voice that says, "I'm not well-developed enough in this area to move forward." Instead, take on a growth mindset. Find ways to focus on the skills where you feel weakest, and improve your overall strength as you move forward.

The second lesson to remember is that your leadership skills are never fully baked. There will never come a time when you have finished learning or growing, or when you have hit "peak proficiency." Skill-building isn't a game that you can win, or a feat you can accomplish. These fundamentals are in a constant state of transition and becoming.

You can always heighten your aptitude and fortify your skill set—and it's up to you to do exactly that.

Discussion Questions

- What do you see as the most compelling way to tell your story? How would you adjust your storytelling technique for different audiences?
- What are examples of when you represented yourself and your cause successfully? What are examples of when you made missteps? What choices could you have made to change your failures into successes?
- What are your strengths as a leader, a representative, and an agent of change? What are your weaknesses? What attributes will you work on, and what skills do you need to source from other people or organizations?

9

Implementation

Key Takeaways

- Before implementation, determine what to measure, set meaningful goals, and develop a timeline for long-term change.
- Reserve time every day to make your work as a citizen statesperson part of your routine.
- Citizen statespeople find careers in government, public service, the nonprofit sector, and the private sector—and interactions between sectors can increase effectiveness.

THERE ARE PLENTY of ways for a citizen statesperson to make an impact. To be effective, though, you need to be able to apply your skills, your passion, and your energy in clear and concrete ways. That might mean building a career in government, in nonprofit work, or in the private sector. It might mean moving between organizations within the same industry, or moving from private industry to government, to nonprofit organizations and back again. No matter what you do, it means taking action.

In this chapter, we discuss how to make your actions effective—by measuring what matters, setting meaningful goals, taking the long view without losing sight of important daily considerations, and applying your skills in a long-term, impactful career.

Measure What Matters

It's an old expression—what gets measured gets done. Measuring something gives you the information you need to take steps towards your goal. It helps clarify your intentions, distilling a broad interest in progress into concrete targets and objectives. It promotes accountability and focus, giving you specific targets to hit and objectives to shoot for while offering information that allows you to make continuous decisions that improve your results. If you're making a case for investments or partnerships, being able to demonstrate how you intend to measure your success will signify your seriousness. Knowing precisely how difficult a goal is to attain will motivate you to achieve it. The word *eustress*—which literally means "good stress"—describes the competitive drive we often feel when we realize that an aspiration is nearly, but not quite, out of reach.

But how do you decide what to measure? How do you determine what's important, and what's not?

Those are real and challenging questions, and the answers are subject to change. For example, economists traditionally measured the wealth of a country by dividing its total economic output by its total population to find its per capita GDP. That calculation was relatively simple, and provided a basic gauge of a country's perceived economic success. Over time, people began to wonder whether wealth—or economic output per citizen—was really the best measure of development. Economic power might be one valuable metric, but what about other factors that contribute to human progress and well-being? To speak to this more comprehensive understanding of development, economists created the Human Development Index (HDI)—a measure that accounts for a population's health, education, and life expectancy, as well as traditional economic indicators.

In the same way, it's important for citizen statespeople to consider the best ways to measure progress in their own endeavors. What will success ultimately look like? What are the steps that are needed to get there? How will you quantify and evaluate improvement?

You may not always get the answers to these questions right. The good news is that the process of thinking about and formulating answers will pay dividends.

For one thing, determining the best way to measure progress encourages you to consider more deeply your approach and objectives. It also helps you make headway with people you are trying to enlist to your cause. In impact investing, for example, there's no set standard for measuring success. Yet marking measures to work toward and being disciplined about setting systems to measure achievements demonstrates to others that you're willing to iterate, you want to improve, and you're curious and motivated about finding an appropriate path forward. In short, you get credit for trying.

Ultimately, setting metrics and measurements helps keep you along the right path, but you don't want to let the measurements you've chosen interfere with you accomplishing your broader mission. Whether you are counting the number of children you taught to brush their teeth or the number of inoculations you were able to provide to people in need, you can't become so attached to any one set of data points that you lose sight of your broader mission. You may find, over time, that you need to deemphasize or drop a metric, or adjust or add one instead. And that's okay! Measurements don't need to be static or set in stone, and you should keep evaluating whether your metrics dovetail with your purpose and values.

At the end of the day, that's the important point. No metric is sacrosanct, but having quantitative values—and demonstrating to people that you keep track of your work—is vital.

Set Meaningful Goals

Part of deciding what to measure involves setting meaningful goals. Goal setting is an important part of citizen statespersonship because it provides a clear target to reach and helps determine which steps to take along the way.

One useful approach to goal setting involves a method that was pioneered 40 years ago by George Doran in a paper about business management: the SMART method.[1] In this case, SMART isn't just a description of the effectiveness of the approach being shouted at you in all-caps; it's also an acronym. And while there are a few different variations of what SMART stands for, the essence is that the goals you set should be specific, measurable, attainable, realistic, and time-bound.

Let's unpack that:

Goals should be specific. Seems reasonable! A vague or general goal doesn't help you move forward because it won't point you in a specific direction. Ask yourself what you want to accomplish, why it's important to you, and what or who will have to be involved. If your proposed goal doesn't have clear answers to those questions, you may have to do work to determine a more precise objective. For example, you might decide that you want to "make the world a better place." That's a nice idea—but what do you need in order to do that? What will success look like? Take time to articulate specific goals that guide you forward.

Goals should be measurable. As we discussed in the previous section, being able to measure progress toward a goal will make you a more effective problem-solver and a more credible changemaker. A measurable goal also offers clear criteria for success, so you'll know when you've achieved your objective (and so will other people). If your goal is to "cut poverty" or "prevent homelessness" or "reduce greenhouse gas emissions," how will you know when you're done? Attach numbers to your efforts that will help you understand how much progress you've made and how much work remains.

Goals should be attainable. It's not helpful to set goals that are such a stretch they are unlikely to be achieved. Want to end world hunger? Great! But is that an attainable goal within the timeframe of this exercise? Probably not. Remember, this is not a visioning exercise to imagine the world in an ideal state; this process is about goal setting to help you implement your work as a citizen statesperson. Consider setting a more achievable goal, like bringing a grocery store to a food desert or establishing a food pantry for a community that needs assistance. Similarly, avoid setting goals that are too easy to achieve; while solving world hunger in the short term might be unrealistic, buying a sandwich for a person on the street is unlikely to make a significant overall impact on the problem. A goal should challenge your abilities, without being so impossible in the short term that it becomes pointless to try.

Goals should be relevant. You need to have a clear idea of your interests and passions so you can make sure your goal matters to you and is clearly related to the issues you care about. If your goals are inconsistent or widely scattered, you'll find yourself moving in all sorts of different directions without coherent purpose. Think about what's important to you—what you consider worthwhile and exciting. Does your goal fit in with those interests? Being a citizen statesperson is not a short-term project—more on that topic in the next section—so you'll want to be sure that the goals you choose are related to topics that keep you curious, motivated, and driven.

Goals should be time-bound. Anyone who has ever worked on a long-term project—like, say, a book—knows that deadlines are important. They help focus our thinking and push us to keep moving forward, even as we encounter other short-term demands on our time and attention. If your goal is open-ended, it's easy to put it on the back burner, or let other interests take priority. Imposing a clear deadline prevents everyday tasks from overwhelming your long-term goal. Creating short-term deadlines within the context of a bigger goal is a strategic way to identify reachable milestones that give you something to grab onto and celebrate as small wins along your great journey of becoming a citizen statesperson.

This approach to goal setting isn't only useful in the context of citizen statespersonship; it's also a helpful tool for charting overarching objectives in your personal and professional life.

Ten years ago, when Carrie was in her mid-20s, she designed a life plan that set out the goals she intended to achieve. It all started when she told her then-boss, now a board member and The Global Good Fund co-founder Knox Singleton, that she wanted to leave her job. At the time, she was working for Knox, who was the CEO at a multibillion-dollar healthcare organization. She had financial stability, benefits, and a path to leadership. Carrie told Knox that she wanted to create a start-up nonprofit organization—a path with very little stability and no benefits, where she would be the leader.

Knox could tell that Carrie was serious. There wasn't any paper on his desk, so he sat her down with a stack of napkins and gave her some of the most helpful advice she had ever received.

"Carrie," he said, "I know that you're ambitious, and I also know that there are things you want to do with your life that will cost money. One way I can support you is by helping you create a life plan to identify the life goals you have and acknowledge up-front how much they will cost to accomplish, both financially and in time."

Carrie was blown away. She was 26 years old at the time, and no one had ever previously explained this concept. She didn't know what a life plan was, but she did know that Knox was right—Carrie had big personal and professional dreams, with no thought-out plans to achieve them. She wanted to find a life partner, but was working nonstop instead of dating. She wanted to raise a family, travel globally, and contribute philanthropically, but she had no intentionality behind how she would handle the financial responsibilities or generate enough money to be effective. She wanted to continue her education and be more focused on her religion, but she hadn't considered how she would devote the time and energy to make these practices priorities.

With Knox's help, Carrie sat down and made a life plan that set out the goals she intended to achieve across five phases of her life. The stages were complete with ages and dates—Phase 1 was ages 26–28; Phase 2 was ages 29–34; Phase 3 was ages 35–44; Phase 4 was ages 45–69; and Phase 5 was age 70 and beyond. Across these five phases, Carrie laid out personal milestones, professional ambitions, and educational objectives along with the financial investments that would be required at each stage. In the decade since, Carrie has continued to use the plan to keep herself on track.

Of course, the plan isn't a static document, and Carrie revisits it every few months to make adjustments and revisions. But simply having this life plan has been a phenomenal exercise in focus, helping her intentionally live the life she wanted to live as a citizen statesperson even before she understood that's what she wanted, and in living a life of social impact before many people understood the topic.

Having a life plan has also helped her say no to opportunities. A few years ago, she began fielding offers from lucrative jobs—a level of compensation that she would never receive in her role at The Global Good Fund. Having a life plan made it easier for her to receive job opportunities, know what she was worth financially based on what the market was willing to pay, refer to her life plan, and decide whether the job opportunities presented aligned with her overall goals, from being present for her children and family to making the world a better place to experiencing global travel on her own terms. Turning down significant sums of money in a vacuum is intensely difficult, but being able to refer to a life plan and say no or yes to opportunities in accordance with an overall strategy has been liberating.

No matter what your own goals might be, from your personal objectives to your professional aims, putting together a clear plan can help you analyze your path with intentionality and hold yourself accountable for results.

Action Item

Formulate a goal that you intend to accomplish, and ensure it is specific, measurable, action-oriented, realistic, and time-bound. Then get to work!

Take the Long View

In part, that's because change takes time. Whether your work takes place in the field of social justice or economic opportunity or foreign policy, it will require navigating a

Citizen statespeople should be prepared to play the long game.

range of institutions and stakeholders often anchored in the status quo. You will have to spend time on preparation, creating a plan for action, and developing a timeline for success. You will need to put that plan into place and make adjustments based on changing circumstances. When you make headway, you will have to maintain that progress, ensuring transformations are durable and effective in the long run.

Some change cannot and should not be rushed. Aligning values, interests, and goals isn't often easy—and it's critical to find the right moment to catalyze a project. Even if you are taking all the right steps in preparation, you may have to wait for outside factors to line up or for favorable circumstances to emerge in order to set your initiative in motion.

The same is true of relationships with people. There are all sorts of reasons why a person might not instantly enlist in your project or initiative. They might be busy or overwhelmed with their own work. They might not immediately see the need for the change you are proposing, or the value of the solutions you propose. They might not have the financial resources to bear at the time that you request them. They might initially disagree with your methods, or they might simply want to wait and learn more before committing to your cause. Building your network is a process, and it needs to be treated like a long-term investment.

Of course, there is a natural inclination to expedite this process, to pitch aggressively and emphatically as soon as you have a person's ear. Opportunities can be rare and fleeting, so it makes sense to embrace momentum whenever and wherever you can. Unfortunately, this approach also risks jeopardizing potential relationships or losing potential support. Instead, you sometimes must let relationships develop at their own pace. Human nature is wired to favor the familiar, and creating a positive relationship with people over time can incline them to support your work in the future. If you can become a familiar face among people who matter to your cause, you can nurture relationships that will move your mission forward.

Not every interaction will bear fruit; in fact, most interactions won't help you achieve your goals right away. But over time, you may find yourself with supporters, mentors, and teammates invested in your success and eager to help you achieve your objectives.

Practice Your Short Game

Playing the long game is necessary, but there are also actions you can take in the short term to strengthen your hand and build your skills as a citizen statesperson. Think of these actions as daily habits that you commit to, and eventually they will become habitualized as a part of your routine.

First, reserve time each day (or at least every other day) for communicating with, preserving, and growing your network.

Take actions daily to check in with people in your circle or to connect with leaders in your issue area. That might mean sending an email to an existing mentor, communicating on LinkedIn with relevant individuals, or scheduling a meeting with an old colleague.

Your relationships won't maintain themselves, and you won't build a following just by sitting back and waiting for people to notice you.

Second, read through the opportunities presented in newsletters and bulletins coming from your network. Is there a conference on a topic that interests you? Is there a workshop that might help you hone your skills or meet new, relevant contacts? Is there a speech or a lecture from a leader in the field that could help you garner a new perspective? Is there a role at an organization that would position you for influence on a topic you care about? The answer to all of these questions is probably yes if you dig beneath the surface and reserve time to develop yourself as a citizen statesperson. Carving out time to invest in yourself is often the hardest part. Organizations and institutions do their part by using emails and newsletters to give updates about everything from public programming to membership benefits to volunteer and professional development opportunities. By informing yourself about available opportunities, you can make decisions about how best to build your skills and influence.

Third, invest—with money!—in opportunities for growth and development. Of course, we recognize that not everyone can afford to plow significant amounts of resources into their favorite causes—but most people can make small, reasonable, targeted investments in their development as a citizen statesperson. That might mean setting aside a small amount of money each day, each week, or each month into a fund for skill-building opportunities or membership dues at an important organization.

There is no "right" amount of money to set aside; it depends on each person's circumstances. What's important is the practice of setting aside a portion of your assets for your personal development. Don't wait until you need the financial resources to start setting aside assets to invest in yourself.

You can also reach out to groups and institutions that sponsor and develop changemakers. By allocating funds and taking steps to secure funding for your efforts on a routine basis, you ensure resources are available when an interesting opportunity arises.

Fourth, promote other emerging citizen statespeople. If a fellowship or event that isn't right for you comes across your desk, take the time to ask yourself whether you know anyone else who would benefit from the experience or make an impact in the role. If you think of a person who might fit the opportunity, reach out and tell them about it. You can even use some of the money you have set aside to support their journey. Taking consistent action to build up other individuals will help you expand and solidify your network, while also exposing talented individuals to platforms and events they might otherwise have missed. Ultimately, mentoring and supporting other nascent citizen statespeople is another great way to make change yourself.

Make It a Career

There are plenty of ways to exercise your interest in citizen statespersonship as part of your long-term career. As a result, you can integrate citizen statespersonship into all sorts of opportunities. Let's dig in!

> *Citizen statespersonship is not an occupation, but an attitude; it's a way of approaching problems and finding solutions.*

Government and Public Service

Government is uniquely positioned to move the needle on certain issues, often by virtue of sheer scale and resources at its disposal. That's why, for citizen statespeople, a career in government can often provide a particularly exciting professional opportunity. Are you interested in environmental resilience? Consider roles in local, state, or federal government that deal with clean energy, public health, or parks and wildlife. Do you have a passion for food security? Look for jobs in federal agencies through the Department of Agriculture or the Department of Health and Human Services, or seek out careers in similar agencies that work with your own community. Are you excited about working in other countries? Government entities like the

State Department and the U.S. Agency for International Development are heavily involved in diplomacy and international support. A job in government can provide an ideal platform to work on issues you care about every day. No matter where you live, there are opportunities to participate in government.

There's also no particular secret to getting these jobs. A citizen statesperson will often find themselves working with various stakeholders, including government officials—and it's natural to come across roles in government and public service that seem fitting or appealing. In some cases, you may already have your eye on a job when it becomes available; in others, your good work may cause another individual from inside the government to tap you on the shoulder and gauge your interest. Even if there is not currently an open position—or if you don't yet feel qualified to apply for the position you want—you can ask yourself how to prepare for seeking the role in the future. Whom would you want to speak with? Whose support might be useful? What would a preliminary step look like? By identifying and demystifying government jobs that seem interesting, you prepare yourself to fill those roles successfully at a later stage.

Another way to become involved in government is to run for public office yourself. Running for office allows you to take a stand for your cause in an entirely new way; to take your case directly to others in your community, and to promote the issues you care about. You can grow your network with political supporters interested in your vision and committed to delivering on your promise. You can amplify your proposals, bringing your priorities to the forefront of your community's civic conversation. From forums like local school boards to city councils to state legislatures and federal offices, getting involved in public service as a candidate is a great way for a citizen statesperson to make an impact—and even if you don't win election on your first try, you will gain valuable experience, contacts, and expertise that will help you succeed in the long run.

Nonprofit Organizations

Of course, serving in government is certainly not the only way to make an impact. Linking with a not-for-profit organization that shares your values can offer extraordinary opportunities to build a career in citizen statespersonship.

One of the benefits of nonprofits is that they require lots of different kinds of skills in service of their mission, so whether you are a marketing genius or a financial guru or a digital media prodigy, you can find a job that leverages your specific talents to make a difference in the world. At the same time, that need for a wide range of skills can also provide a chance to try new things. Nonprofits typically rely on a smaller team of individuals to handle the workload, which means that each individual employee will probably take on a variety of different tasks. You may enter employment at a nonprofit with skills in communication or development or policy design, but you will likely leave with experience in research, grant-writing, event planning, and all sorts of other interesting undertakings and endeavors. For a citizen statesperson who is eager to learn, nonprofits can be valuable settings for education and growth.

Some nonprofit organizations and institutions offer training initiatives to help connect enthusiastic and talented people with aligned experiences. American citizen engagement opportunities like Fulbright scholarships and Peace Corps programs help organize motivated individuals to go to other parts of the world and make a difference. Other countries have built similar public engagement programs that replicate these approaches abroad through initiatives like Germany's Goethe Institute or the British

Council. In many cases, public engagement has become more fluid than ever before; rather than a one-way or bilateral flow of information, we see a globalized flow of best practices, in which communities and countries share what works with one another, and help export and implement good ideas around the world. That's the context in which citizens statespeople operate today—and it offers an extraordinary variety of chances to take part.

The Private Sector

It's relatively straightforward to understand how citizen statespeople can make an impact in government and nonprofit environments. Those sectors are inherently mission driven, and offer plenty of opportunities for selfless contributions to the world around us. But what if you're interested in the private sector? What if it's important to you to make money, or to build a business? What if you are drawn to the corporate world's fast pace and drive for innovation? Can you still be an effective citizen statesperson?

Of course!

Ted Levinson is an example of an individual who is doing good through private-sector work. For 10 years, Levinson worked in a corporate financing and banking role, providing financing and advising for some of Northern California's most well-known industries. In 2008, he spent time leading his own startup company, getting a feel for the nuts and bolts of entrepreneurship—and by the end of that year, he had transitioned into a role at a financial services organization that worked to connect social entrepreneurs with capital. Today, he leads his own impact investing debt fund, called Beneficial Returns, which provides loans for social enterprises focused on sustainable agriculture and energy, waste reduction, and poverty alleviation. The company is making a profit while also supporting the growth of social enterprises that operate in emerging markets.

The truth is that the two often go hand-in-hand—something that boards of directors and CEOs of large companies are beginning to recognize. In 2019, for example, the CEO of BlackRock, Larry Fink wrote the following in a letter to fellow CEOs:[2]

> *Citizen statespeople aren't required to take a vow of poverty. There's no shame in doing well and doing good at the same time.*

Profits are in no way inconsistent with purpose—in fact, profits and purpose are inextricably linked. Profits are essential if a company is to effectively serve all of its stakeholders over time—not only shareholders, but also employees, customers, and communities. Similarly, when a company truly understands and expresses its purpose, it functions with the focus and strategic discipline that drive long-term profitability. Purpose unifies management, employees, and communities. It drives ethical behavior and creates an essential check on actions that go against the best interests of stakeholders. Purpose guides culture, provides a framework for consistent decision-making, and, ultimately, helps sustain long-term financial returns for the shareholders of your company. . . .

One thing, however, is certain: the world needs your leadership. As divisions continue to deepen, companies must demonstrate their commitment to the countries, regions, and communities where they operate, particularly on issues central to the world's future prosperity. Companies cannot solve every issue of public importance, but there are

many—from retirement to infrastructure to preparing
workers for the jobs of the future—that cannot be solved
without corporate leadership.

Companies are beginning to put money behind this approach.
Large technology companies like Salesforce rotate their
executives through fellowships with the World Economic Forum
to better understand the societal challenges we face as we enter
the fourth industrial revolution. At Google and Pfizer, employees
can take sabbaticals to volunteer in alternative settings and apply
their skillsets toward furthering a good cause while benefiting
from a different, socially impactful perspective. At the Federal
Reserve Bank, senior executives can rotate through the Bill &
Melinda Gates Foundation to explore how lending mechanisms
can transform communities.

The point is that citizen statespeople are not only using private
sector resources to do good work; they're also creating
opportunities to infuse private sector companies, executives, and
employees with purpose and principles.

Connecting the Dots

Contrary to common belief, these roles are not exclusive.
Beginning a career in government, nonprofit advocacy, or
corporate citizenship doesn't preclude you from changing sectors
later in your career. In fact, a job in any of these fields will offer
you experiences that serve you well in other sectors and industries.
Working in government will help you understand policymaking
and bureaucracy. Spending time in the private sector teaches
invaluable lessons about how to motivate individual actors to
take action for the public good. Working in a nonprofit capacity
helps build deep expertise in an issue area, and puts you in touch

with a variety of motivated groups and individuals who will assist you as you continue your journey.

We're not the only people who recognize this reality. Plenty of other leaders see the value in hiring individuals from the nonprofit sector to work in government, or bringing people with government experience into the private sector, or shifting private sector leaders into either of the other two areas. That kind of movement can help you turn a career in one sector or industry into a very different opportunity for citizen statespersonship.

Samantha Power, for example, began her career in the nonprofit sector, working first at the Carnegie Endowment for International Peace and later as the leader of the Carr Center for Human Rights Policy at Harvard University's Kennedy School of Government. As a prominent and well-respected policy expert, she was tapped to serve in then-Senator Barack Obama's office in a foreign policy fellow role, and became a senior foreign policy advisor to his presidential campaign. Fifteen years later, she has served as a member of the U.S. National Security Council, U.S. Ambassador to the United Nations, and the Administrator of the United States Agency for International Development.

Stories like this one aren't just examples of how a person in one line of work can transition to another; they are also reminders that citizen statespeople can be found everywhere, with diverse backgrounds that help them understand the connective tissues between and among government, nonprofits, and the private sector. When citizen statespeople exist in the private sector, the public sector, and nonprofit organizations at the same time, there are more opportunities for productive connections in all directions because all parties are more interested in fluid interplay. Citizen statespeople in government can use their convening power and resources to make progress, while nonprofit leaders can provide expertise and long-range planning, and private-sector individuals can spur innovation and discovery. By placing citizen statespeople in all these different arenas, we can create a virtuous cycle that improves collaboration and encourages the best ideas to rise to the top.

Ultimately, society needs as many smart, experienced, creative people engaged in the civic, dialogue, and policy process as possible, from every angle. With more smart voices, we can gain more incisive, diverse, and useful perspectives. With more dialogue among motivated and thoughtful individuals, we can develop better and more effective solutions. More interactions between citizen statespeople lead to better policy, better governance, and better results.

Discussion Questions

- What goals you are trying to achieve?
- What does success look like? How will you measure your growth and development?
- What steps will you take, in the short term and the long term, to make progress towards your goals?

Notes

1. George T. Doran, "There's a SMART way to write management's goals and objectives." *Management Review* 70, no. 11 (1981): 35–36.
2. "Profit & Purpose," Larry Fink's 2019 letter to CEOs, https://www.blackrock.com/americas-offshore/en/2019-larry-fink-ceo-letter.

10

Who We Are

> **Key Takeaways**
>
> - Look for connections between people, ideas, and initiatives—and use those connections to be effective in making change.
> - Lean into opportunities to make an impact—and don't be put off by goals that have never been achieved before.
> - You will fail more times than you succeed, but your successes will shine brighter, creating more opportunities to achieve impact.

Be a Connector: Carrie Rich's Story

We are often taught to become the best at one thing, to dig our own trench, to stay in our own silo, and to focus on our task. That's one way to succeed—but that's not what I did. I'm not the best businessperson. I'm not the best writer. I'm not the most successful person who's ever founded a nonprofit. When I was co-captain of my high school track team, I wasn't even the fastest runner. I can't tell you how to be the best at any of those things.

Having interests in different areas—and being willing to see how people, ideas, and industries are connected—helped create a global network of social entrepreneurs with millions of beneficiaries around the world.

Let's back up. I started off as a kid in the suburbs of Boston, Massachusetts, with two parents employed by the federal government—not exactly the risk-taking types. Things were about as stable as they could get. Other kids have stories about their parents taking a job that took them across the country or around the world. When I was one year old, my family moved into the house next door. That was the closest we got to upheaval. My upbringing gave me a strong appreciation for community. I knew growing up that I wanted to do something driven by my values. From an early age, I was interested in systems and connections and how people interact.

When I was 16, I attended a summer program at Georgetown University in Washington, D.C., for high school students who wanted to be doctors. Those of us in the program rotated between different stations that were supposed to help maintain or restore a person's health, including a food pantry, funded partly by grants from the city, where we'd serve food to some of the poorest people in the District of Columbia. I remember seeing a man from my table get up from his seat, walk outside, and use a special pass from a city aid agency to get on a bus. That night, after we had shifted to our hospital rotation, I saw that same man walk into the emergency room and collapse from chronic illness and exhaustion.

It was clear to me that the system that had taken this human being from a food pantry to the bus to the emergency room wasn't working. It wasn't enough for me to learn about being just one part of the system. There was something wrong with how the pieces of the system fit together. I wanted to understand what was wrong, and why the system was broken. I went home and told my parents I wasn't going to be a surgeon—I was going to learn how to run hospitals.

That's what I did. While attending Lehigh University, I majored in an interdisciplinary degree that hardly any other students pursued. I showed up for several classes in an auditorium-style room, and not a single other student was in the classes! Luckily, instead of canceling the classes that held my interest, my professors asked me to meet independently for several hours weekly, assigned books to read, and taught me one on one using the Socratic method (until eventually one other student joined). My professors required that I go into the community to see how the world worked, which I did, volunteering at Federally Qualified Health Centers and the local hospital. It was quite the educational experience.

Though no degree existed at the time to focus my studies on the health of society, I wrote a letter to the then-president of the university detailing why degree offerings that focused on the public's health and health systems were relevant to the future, and I pulled together a mock-up health major based on existing classes and professors. I understood that putting in the work to pitch these ideas would not benefit me personally, but I imagined that future Lehigh students, and ultimately the world, would benefit. I graduated, traveled independently to India and Tanzania doing my own version of health-focused study abroad, and returned to Georgetown University to pursue a graduate degree in health administration, the same place where I'd figured out several summers earlier that our system was broken. The connections kept coming.

If I was going to learn about healthcare, I wanted to understand everything I could, from the drugs we administer to the public health we deliver (or don't) to the health facilities we maintain to the way we train health professionals. In addition to graduate school studies, I took a training course on how to teach. I wrote papers on healthcare sustainability, and was eventually asked to design and lead a class on the topic of health sustainability attended by law students, medical students, and nurses. If I was going to teach about sustainability, I figured I should know about broader sustainability infrastructure in healthcare facilities, so I organized conferences on the topic that brought more than a hundred health administrators and healthcare company CEOs to Georgetown University from across the country.

Beginning in college, I had a habit of approaching interesting strangers for 15 minutes of advice, asking them a list of ten questions, including "Who is the most creative person you've ever met?" One of the people I spoke with said that the most creative person she had ever met was a woman named Tama Duffy Day, who lived in Washington, D.C., and was a designer for a leading international architecture firm. While I was studying health administration, the United States was spending $250 billion on health facility infrastructure across the country, and I wasn't learning anything about the topic in school, so I contacted Tama Duffy Day, and asked if I could work for her to learn about design.

Tama asked, "Are you a designer?"

I said, "No."

She asked, "Are you an architect?"

I said, "No."

She asked, "Why should I hire you?"

I said, "Because I can be the liaison between the designers and the administrators who are making the decisions. I can be the connector."

And she said, "Yes."

This all happened during graduate school. To complete my master's degree, I was required to partake in an internship, which

I spent working for the Chief Operating Officer (COO) at a local health system called Inova. But when the COO left the organization halfway through my internship, I needed to find another role. They put me to work mopping floors, pushing the snack cart, folding laundry in the maternity ward where I would later give birth to our children, and taking attendance—which meant that everyone who walked in the door had to introduce themselves to me.

One day, who should walk in but Knox Singleton, the CEO of the entire health system at that time. I thought, what would make a CEO of a multibillion-dollar health system talk to me? I figured everyone talked to the CEO of a health system about healthcare, so I decided to talk with him about living a life of purpose and building a legacy. I connected with his assistant by figuring out email formatting through LinkedIn, made an appointment, and had a conversation with him about his work building health systems in Haiti, about his goals and ambitions, and about how to pursue a mission-driven life. I didn't want the conversation to end. So when I ran out of things to say, I blurted out, "Would you write a book with me?" And to my utter shock, he said, "Sure." We found a third co-author (who had more sense about how to write a book!), and for the next three years, the three of us wrote a book about health sustainability, *Sustainability for Healthcare Management: A Leadership Imperative*. The book went on to become a top five business book in the German business newspaper *Handelsblatt*.

So now we're in the middle of it all. I'd recently completed graduate school and was writing articles for peer-reviewed journals. I was teaching a class on healthcare sustainability, and organizing national conferences on the topic. I was working for a leading international architecture firm to understand health facility infrastructure from a design perspective. I was writing a book with the CEO of a multibillion-dollar health system. Connecting had been good. Life was good. But here's the thing: one of the reasons it's tempting to stay in our lane is that when we step outside, plenty of people are waiting to try to force us back. That's a lesson I learned the hard way.

One day, when I was working at the architecture firm, I received a message from the staff at a journal. The professor at Georgetown University who had been advising me had accused me of plagiarizing an article that we'd co-authored and submitted together. She wanted my name removed from the article. I was crestfallen. How could my mentor, the person I'd spent every Wednesday afternoon with, think I'd do that?

Since that time, I've learned that when people attack others, they almost always genuinely believe they are right. The realization that other people have just as much conviction in their beliefs or their motivations as I have in mine has helped me move forward in the face of immense difficulty.

That's what I know now. But back then? I was devastated. I had trusted and respected this person as a mentor and a friend, and she had made up an accusation of plagiarism to knock me down.

I may not agree with or even understand a person's views, but I know what it's like to fight for something I believe in, so I can at least tolerate in an empathetic way when someone disagrees with me, or even attacks me.

Meanwhile, at Inova, I was being given responsibility for things I didn't know how to do. I had a tremendous sponsor in my boss, who gave me the platform, resources, and mentorship I needed to thrive. I was in my early 20s, advancing when other people weren't. That led to a formal appeal to overturn my promotion, made by frustrated colleagues who were not getting promoted. The human resources and legal departments got involved and I dealt with several reputational blows and sticky notes with nasty messages left on my desk from forces of the status quo around gender, age, and the nature of being a change agent.

It didn't matter that I had spent years building a solid reputation. It only mattered that people with an axe to grind were trying to take it all away. At that point, I could have walked away. I could have left Inova and found some other job with a fresh start. I could've left Georgetown University and hid from the accusations coming from someone I had trusted and respected. But I didn't do any of those things. I had spent my life until that point looking for connections—between people, organizations, and ideas. I had been focused on how systems related to each other, and how one area of research, study, or activity inevitably interacted with others.

One of the realities about being a connector is that it helped me see how I was connected—connected to the topics that mattered, and to the values I cared about.

I was part of a bigger set of ideas, principles, and outcomes that were important to me. It wasn't just about my reputation or my career—it was about my ability to do good, to work for progress, and to help build the kind of world I cared about.

Taking me on was one thing, but I wasn't going to let petty people set back the work that I knew needed to be done. I requested a hearing at Georgetown University, which was never granted. I participated in an investigation at Inova, which happened. I continued my work. I stayed focused on my objectives, and stayed connected to my values and my goals. In short, I kept going.

When I was 25, I told Knox, my boss in healthcare, about an idea. I told him I was lucky to work for him—but I also understood that there were a lot of great young people with strong values who don't get to work for the head of a multibillion-dollar organization who cares about investing in emerging leaders.

I said, "Why don't we find people like me who have strong work ethic, a moral compass, and are using their lives for good, and connect them with people like you who have business success and hearts of gold, and put targeted capital behind that pairing as a catalyst for good?"

He said, "That sounds great—now please get back to doing your job."

But Knox didn't forget our conversation. In fact, he spent considerable time reflecting on the value of our mentor-mentee relationship and using it as a basic premise for how to scale social impact. Through many brainstorming conversations, we conceived of these concepts behind The Global Good Fund:

- Leaders are the secret sauce in making real social impact.
- The most effective way to accelerate the development of high-potential young leaders is to replicate our relationship, or in Knox's words, "find high-performing young talent and focus on accelerating their development through the mentorship of a corporate executive."

For my 26th birthday, Knox gave me a card with a quote from the 18th-century theologian John Wesley, who founded the most well-known independent Methodist movement that continues to this day. The birthday card read:

Do all the good you can,
By all the means you can,
In all the ways you can,
In all the places you can,
At all the times you can,
To all the people you can,
As long as ever you can.

In the card was a hundred dollars and a note that read, "This is the money I would've spent taking you and your colleagues out for pizza on your birthday. Take it, and live out this admonition." I wrote to my friends and family. I told them, "My boss gave me lunch money. Here is what six great organizations I've volunteered with could do if we turned a hundred dollars into a thousand dollars for each of them." My friends and family sent lunch money and coffee change to make a difference—but it wasn't enough. So I kept going.

I contacted the people who had been in my high school, and classmates from college and graduate school. I emailed colleagues from my time working in design—including Tama Duffy Day, the most creative person one leader had ever met. I reached out to all the people who had responded to my 10 questions, my colleagues, family, and friends who had supported my professional work and personal growth. I even connected with the people I had gotten to know during hard times: the members of the Inova board who had seen me fight back against rumors, and the men and women at Georgetown University who had watched me refuse to back down when someone I had respected tried to derail my career.

I contacted each of these people by email with a subject line that read, "The Global Good Fund." I didn't think too hard about the title, because I didn't know it would mean anything, but I knew that the idea of connecting entrepreneurs for social good with the resources and people to broaden their scope was an idea worth exploring. It worked. People started sending money, and then more money, and then more money. Soon I had more coming in than I knew what to do with—more than a thousand dollars, more than five thousand dollars.

Knox once told me that people help people they like. Life has taught me that's true—when friends and acquaintances and near-strangers were sending me money, they weren't just investing in my idea; they were investing in me. People sent money because they knew me, they believed in me, and they recognized that I was going to think beyond myself to generate an idea that was interesting, that was different, and, hopefully, that worked.

Meanwhile, Knox and I continued working together to define the core concept behind The Global Good Fund and bring it to action through the creation and building of the organization, which required tremendous collaboration over several years. We ultimately raised $2 million between the two of us and together, we turned that hundred dollars for pizza money into a global social enterprise.

Thanks primarily to Knox's leadership, we built a board, and the board—filled with some of the same people who had seen me fight back against attacks and challenging circumstances—asked me to run the organization.

That's where The Global Good Fund came from. I went from wanting to improve the health of one patient to trying to improve the health of a hospital system to attempting to improve the health of the world. And it was the connections I made—through success and failure, through hard work and long hours—that made it possible. I didn't become the best at one thing. To this day, I'm not the best at anything. I didn't stick to digging my trench. Instead, I was a connector. I connected subjects and ideas and people and organizations. I recognized how systems interacted, and how bigger machines could be built out of interlocking parts.

Today, The Global Good Fund helps make those connections for other young leaders by connecting ideas, people, resources, and opportunities to do good. The Global Good Fund's cumulative impact includes 3,000 permanent jobs created in underserved communities, 200 entrepreneurs served in 40 countries, over 50,000 global community members, $150 million raised by the entrepreneurs, and nearly 10 million lives positively impacted. Here's how it works. We search the world for extraordinary people who have started a socially impactful company and sustained it for between two and five years. These are people who have already taken a dive out of the airplane and are building a parachute on the way down. They're smart, they're values-driven, and they're coachable. What they're not yet is as connected as they could be to the people and the resources that can help them grow.

We put out a call to these social entrepreneurs, and we receive over 3,000 applicants every year from people who aspire to be Global Good Fund Fellows. We engage many volunteers so that four people review each application. We conduct video interviews, board member interviews, and staff interviews. We filter through their applications for six months of due diligence, with as much time and intensity as they would get from any venture capital firm looking to invest. But instead of investing in their business, we invest in *the person* as an individual.

We want to know: Regardless of what your business is today, do you have the fire in your eye and the hunger in your belly to make the world a better place? Eventually, we narrow our application pool to a handful of fellows. We do a virtual onboarding, and a leadership assessment that we created ourselves—and that we now offer to other prestigious organizations and entrepreneurs looking to measure and improve their own leadership.

We pair each Global Good Fund Fellow with a leadership coach who helps the entrepreneur create a personalized leadership plan, tailored directly to the individual. And at an annual summit, we connect our fellows with business mentors and coaches—people who have run $40 million to $60 billion companies, and who are looking to translate business success into social significance. We give $10,000 philanthropic grants to each Global Good Fund Fellow to implement their leadership plans, and we connect them with our network—mentors and alumni of the program to keep them involved, strengthen their connections, and invest in their success.

It works. In January 2019, Emory University completed an independent assessment of the programmatic impact of The Global Good Fund as measured by the short-term commercial performance of Global Good Fund Fellows, evenly split between fellows based in the U.S. and emerging markets. The study was led and conducted by professors at Emory University's Goizueta School of Business, funded by the Kauffman Foundation. The Global Good Fund Fellows outperformed the benchmark peer group comprising participants in 52 other accelerator programs that are part of the Global Accelerator Learning Initiative. Specifically, The Global Good Fund Fellows raised more than double the capital to scale their businesses for impact, as compared to social entrepreneurs in the control group. That's the power of investing in individual leadership and helping individuals without an established platform forge connections to live their potential. We established a link between investing in personal development and expected outcomes in leadership development, enterprise growth, and social impact.

Eventually we at The Global Good Fund realized we were sitting on 10,000 vetted social entrepreneurs. We were helping accelerate the social impact of these incredible individuals, investing in their leadership potential, de-risking their companies, and then handing them off to venture capital firms that invested in their businesses. So we decided to do both, and now I run an impact fund—Global Impact Fund II—that invests for market-leading financial returns in socially conscious organizations with a focus on underrepresented entrepreneurs, especially women, Black, and Brown entrepreneurs, taking equity in their businesses to help them scale; this model supports creating a sustainable revenue stream so that we continue to build connections, invest in leaders, and drive lasting, positive impact.

That's what The Global Good Fund does—it expands the circle outward, and encourages people to see how they connect to the world around them and how they can use that connection to make a difference in their field. Individual development ripples out to enterprise growth, which ripples out to social impact. That's why it's called "*social* good"—it's about connections among people, among communities, among organizations and companies and societies.

Recently I received a note from the interim dean of Lehigh University's College of Health. She wrote: "Even before I took on this role, I have admired (via LinkedIn) the work of The Global Good Fund. I think the health goals that you articulate align with a significant part of the work that our faculty and students are and will be doing as the College grows, specifically, by improving lives through better understanding the multiple determinants of health. . . . I have to admit that part of my thinking is influenced by what I know of your time at Lehigh, when you were advocating Lehigh's leadership for more interdisciplinary programs that would prepare graduates for the 'real world.' When I was working with a faculty group to propose the Health, Medicine, and Society program, we cited your letter to the president as evidence of student demand for a health-focused interdisciplinary program. You probably know that it is now one of the most popular majors on campus. I also remember your coming to campus to speak on a panel with students about public-focused work in health. Now that we have a College of Health at Lehigh, the possibilities are even greater for expanding on your early vision."

Today, I am humbled to serve on the Dean's Advisory Council for the College of Health at Lehigh University. I also joined the board of directors of Trinity Health, one of the largest not-for-profit, Catholic healthcare systems in the nation, with 115,000 colleagues and nearly 26,000 physicians and clinicians caring for diverse communities across 25 states. Headquartered in Livonia, Michigan, its annual operating revenue is $20.2 billion with $1.2 billion returned to its communities in the form of charity care and other community benefit programs.

When I was learning about hospital administration, or working on a book, or meeting with designers and CEOs and philanthropists, did I know the full extent of what I was building? No, I can't say I did. Did I know how it would all fit together?

> *It can feel like baby steps, but baby steps are good if you're taking them in a positive direction—even if that direction is just "outward."*

I did not. But I knew then what I still know now: that being more connected to the causes and people I care about, and understanding how those topics relate to each other, drives extraordinary, expansive impact.

That's my story. I started as a kid in the Boston suburbs, and today I help lead multiple global organizations. But I'm not special. I'm not the best businessperson. I'm not the best writer. I'm not the best leader of a nonprofit organization. I'm still not the best runner. I have never become the best at anything I've done. And I've faced challenges that set me back.

Ultimately, it was being able to see in 360 degrees that kept me moving forward. It was understanding how everything fit together that kept it all from falling apart. And it was the connections I made—with people, ideas, and causes—that make me who I am, that have fueled other entrepreneurs to live their potential as citizen statespeople, sending ripples around the globe. Those connections have—hopefully—made the world a better place.

Seek Challenges and Create Opportunities:
Dean Fealk's Story

I was born and raised in a modest and bucolic suburb of Detroit. My father, a psychiatrist, is one of the most open-minded and forward-thinking people I know, with an abiding view of the human condition that we all have more in common than what sets us apart. My mother, a retired 30-year elementary school teacher and early proponent of bringing STEAM education—science, technology, engineering, art, and math—to young children, loved to engage young minds and inspire her students. My parents communicated high expectations of achievement without ever overtly pushing me and my sister. Hard work and self-sufficiency were encouraged. By the time I turned 18, I had learned the value of a hard-earned dollar, working a variety of part-time jobs alongside people from all walks of life as a parking valet, waiter, retail sales clerk, and coffee packager.

My interest in politics and policy was catalyzed during my university years, when I had the good fortune and opportunity to intern in the office of a state senator, Jackie Vaughn III, a long-time senior state legislator in Michigan. Senator Vaughn had marched in the civil rights movement, met Bobby Kennedy, authored landmark state civil rights legislation, and authored the bill to establish Martin Luther King Day in Michigan. "I've been to the top of the mountain," he would say. He brought those combined experiences to bear in his work and acquitted himself with extraordinary dignity and self-effacing modesty. He listened attentively to everyone who visited his book-lined office, whether constituents, grizzled political veterans, or 19-year-old interns. This made a significant and lasting impression on me.

Senator Vaughn himself took a unique opportunity early in his career to study in England as a Marshall Scholar—an honor especially rare for an African American of his generation. That opportunity afforded him broad, open-minded perspective. When I worked for him, he encouraged me to explore life outside the United States, because he believed in a cosmopolitan mindset to draw from a fuller sense of ideas and solutions for public policy challenges.

At his encouragement, I also went to graduate school in the United Kingdom. The diverse student body and community exposed me to a broad array of disparate viewpoints. My thinking grew and expanded. Many of my embedded assumptions were challenged or upended. Just as importantly, I developed a taste for exploring the world outside of my comfort zone, and I decided I wanted to spend time studying in Asia, a focus of my graduate studies. But I was also determined to become a lawyer to play a greater role in the policy conversation I had been exposed to during time in state politics. So I applied to study as a Fulbright Scholar in Asia—and promptly forgot about the application, moved back to San Francisco, and started law school. Then one day many months later, I received a letter informing that I had been selected to teach and study in Korea for a year.

In law school, many students focus on a relatively narrow and prescribed path, and I was no different. My initial instinct was perhaps to turn down the opportunity, and refrain from taking time off. I consulted with the dean of the law school, thinking she would talk me out of a detour to an exotic port of call. I figured she would say, "Playtime is over. Do you want to become a lawyer or not?" Instead, what she said was, "Law school isn't going anywhere. Do you want to expand your horizons and international perspectives or not?" I was surprised—and went looking for a second opinion. I brought the same question to a law professor I respected immensely, and asked what he thought about this life decision. He advised, "Business and professional life pivot on relationships. So go to Korea and build meaningful and enduring relationships." It was the advice I needed to hear: that my attractions to travel and international experiences were more than just wanderlust, that they had value and virtue, and that time spent outside of law school, and the traditional prescribed path, could be both personally and professionally enriching. I packed my bag, put law school on hold for a year, and went to Korea as a Fulbright Scholar.

En route to a new adventure, I somehow developed the notion that I wanted to serve as the first American to clerk at the Constitutional Court of Korea—the equivalent of the United States Supreme Court. I was not sure if this ambition flowed from a semblance of youthful pioneer spirit or my instinctive attraction to head directly to the "source" of action. I entered the country on a prestigious scholarship, but I didn't know anyone or how the court worked. I was nonetheless able to make some important connections in Seoul by taking law classes there, and in doing so a well-established law professor took an interest in me and asked about my career ambitions after law school. I explained that I envisioned myself working in U.S. politics with a focus on Korean issues and that I felt if I could develop the tools needed to live out that ambition, then I could be successful in my career aspirations. On the strength of the idea I had shared, my law professor recommended me to the Constitutional Court of Korea. I became the first American to clerk there. It was a tremendous and eye-opening experience, and it taught me the value of visualizing a specific goal—one that takes you directly to the "source," and articulating to others the purpose of and merits of that goal.

It's like climbing a rock wall that leads to greater heights. The Fulbright ethos was resonant educational pedagogy for my journey. Its spirit and values have remained among the most impactful influences in my life. The first two months I spent in Korea, we studied the (amazing!) people, history, culture,

> *Part of career jujitsu is that describing your aspirations and ambitions to people is inspirational; it encourages others to help you translate your ideas into concrete stepping-stones.*

and language of Korea. Ultimately, it was all about building ties between two countries and its people; at its core, it engendered mutual respect. That experience resonated with me—and it's the reason why I continued to pursue future experiences, to go beyond being a lost foreigner, and to embark on missions to promote friendship, understanding, and commonalities among people from different backgrounds. I felt the same way years later on the Marshall Memorial Fellowship to Europe, the U.S.-Spain Young Leaders Program, and the Eisenhower Fellowship in China. You don't have to win a prestigious fellowship to serve as a goodwill ambassador or find commonalities with others. As a professor of mine once remarked, "If you see awards preceded by the word 'prestigious,' it means no one has heard of them."

The spirit behind the accolades is what's important: to go somewhere with a truly open mind and open heart, and strive to be your own best representative.

At the completion of the Fulbright Scholarship, I returned to finish my legal studies. But the experience overseas and its impact stayed with me—so much so, in fact, that in relatively short order, I moved back to Asia to work as an attorney in one of the region's largest law firms and as a consultant to the World Bank. In terms of willingness to try new things, I was spending much of my time working on corporate transactions, including mergers and acquisitions, which were considered among the most coveted areas for a young lawyer to practice. Meanwhile, I was being approached repeatedly to get involved in Korean employment law issues. I assumed that Korean employment law would be narrow, and that focusing on such a specific topic might signal the early demise of my career, but when I finally said yes, it turned out that those issues were incredibly important to companies investing in Korea. I soon found myself as a go-to advisor to several major multinational corporate clients. When I had been focused on mergers and acquisitions (M&A) that was considered sexier work, my interlocutors were closer to my level—relatively junior. By contrast, when I was engaged in the less sexy work off the beaten path, I was directly interacting with local CEOs of major corporations.

Later, when it came time to transition back to the United States, it was this range of experiences that allowed me to land a position at an international law firm in Silicon Valley.

At that time, the international law practice in Silicon Valley was, in many ways, still somewhat parochial. Firms saw the Bay Area as the center of the tech world, but didn't necessarily understand the challenges clients faced on the ground in disparate geographies. For this reason, my exposure and experience "on the other end," having practiced abroad, became valuable for translating culture, business objectives, and regulatory challenges.

The experience taught me not to blindly follow the pack, but rather to remain willing to experiment with new things, even when the value of the experiences may not be immediately evident.

Along the way, I developed the "law of the other"—an approach that I had pieced together from observing a pioneering American lawyer in Korea, who became one of the most successful foreign lawyers in the country. He gained the confidence of many Korean business leaders on the basis that he understood the objectives of foreign investors and executives from the United States and Europe. At the same time, he convinced the American multinational companies and investors that he understood the mindset of Korean culture and thinking necessary to thrive in the country.

Broadly, I sought to develop a professional identity as an international lawyer—but I also wanted to develop a reputation as someone deeply engaged in politics

When you have more than one identity to draw from (which, as eclectic citizen statespeople, we invariably do!), you decide which are the most potent to lead with and underscore.

and policy. Often, the qualities you highlight are the ones scarcest in a given context. For example, if you attend a conference of international lawyers, an identity as an international lawyer will not easily distinguish. But if you set yourself apart from the thousand other people in the room as a policy or leadership expert, you suddenly become more interesting. If, the following week, you participate in an event geared towards policy leaders, you can consider underscoring your identity as an international lawyer and stand out on that basis. To be clear, even if you were never the most prominent in either category to begin with— international lawyer or policy or leadership expert—the combination of those two facets can coalesce to make you more interesting and memorable in a way that focusing on just one of these dimensions rarely would.

As a recent expatriate returnee from Asia, I found out that political life in the United States is porous and relatively open to newcomers. I became involved in my first presidential campaign not long after returning Stateside. I then took time off from my private practice to campaign in Iowa and also became more deeply involved in California politics. I discovered that my law practice was a great platform for pursuing other interests. I had a reason to be in any room, both because lawyers are involved in just about every kind of civic and public policy project, and also because lawyers are typically open to finding their next high-quality client. I quickly learned that indeed the private practice of law was a rich platform for doing what I wanted to do. Too little civic and political engagement, and I really didn't find my professional life fully engaging or interesting. Too much, and I was spread too thin in my law practice.

I discovered that if one was in corporate America and wanted to become a citizen statesperson, one could often find a way to speak for one's company or organization in promoting a project or issue. The product had better clearly align—in other words, the product needed to be a market fit. Lawyers themselves are ultimately their own product; they sell themselves. I found that reality liberating. If the issue touched on international trade, investment, or regulation, then my legal expertise might prove helpful. If the issue related to financial services, clients still needed a lawyer. The legal platform was broad enough that I could pick and choose the activities in which I was interested. I learned to think about the ways I could leverage my touch point organizations and affiliations and build a personal platform alongside my more focused professional platform.

At the same time, I became increasingly interested in corporate leadership and the role corporations play as stakeholders in solving broader societal and global problems. I became involved with the leading industry organizations in the region and state, including the Bay Area Council and Silicon Valley Leadership Group, and California Business Roundtable, serving in leadership roles and on their boards of directors. I quickly found that through one opportunity, I invariably met interesting people and more opportunities presented themselves. My civic activities led to further political opportunities, at the state, national, and international level. I joined trade and investment delegations representing the state of California around the world. By being authentic to my interests, understanding why businesses make the decisions they make, and studying how they can be more impactful in their communities, I forged connections and made an impact much greater than I would have imagined.

Membership in these kinds of groups lent credibility to pursue additional leadership experiences. When I interviewed for premier national or international leadership development opportunities, such as Eisenhower Fellowships or Presidential Leadership Scholars or the German Marshall Fund's Marshall

Memorial Fellowship, I told the narratives of my prior leadership experiences. I parlayed one strength to lend credibility to succeeding in a different realm. There were synergies not necessarily obvious at face value.

I also discovered that leading business and civic organizations valued a (relatively) young voice perhaps more liberal or open-minded than many of the CEOs. I was able to demonstrate that I was level-headed, yet brought a different voice and viewpoint—largely due to my international and cross-sector experiences—to conversations, whether discussing housing, regional transportation, environmental issues, or international trade. I was not reticent to be the only proponent of an idea in the room, in some cases, and I always tried to comport myself in an open-minded way, so that when it was my turn to be a needed contrarian, or even speak truth to power, I would be paid the same courtesy. People knew that if I said something they disagreed with, it wasn't because I had a hidden agenda or was a jerk; I could disagree with the CEO of a large company and still have them invite me to dinner with their family the following week. I found that when I was thoughtful in the way that I interacted with people and presented my ideas, I could disagree without being disagreeable, and play a role in moving broader issues forward in the process.

As I gained traction within these networks, I realized I wanted to start convening leaders on international issues. In seeking substantial opportunities to do that, I noticed that there was an interest in relationships between the United States and the European Union, so I partnered with a dynamic leader named Michael Fernandez to form an organization we called Transatlantic West to attract EU leaders to northern California. We saw an opportunity and filled a void hosting heads of state, ministers, and other political leaders from around Europe for discussions with California business and civic leaders. As our success attracted attention, we became increasingly better known as a platform for non-EU leaders; we went on to expand our remit to host leaders from Asia and Latin America. These activities developed synergies with other leadership activities, including the business community, because many business leaders wanted to get involved. They sought to expand their horizons and join a conversation with leaders they might not otherwise intersect with. Just because you're a well-known tech CEO, for example, doesn't mean you have the opportunity to speak with the attorney general of India.

I count myself as fortunate to pursue a wide variety of experiences and to learn a great deal from extraordinary mentors. I have learned to home in on the source—ground zero—to step outside of my comfort zone, that the most difficult path is often the most rewarding, and that if the forum or platform you seek doesn't exist, you can construct it yourself. I have developed the law of the other: to underscore the unique aspects of your skillset or background depending on the context. And I have learned that intentionally and purposefully dedicating part of your professional time and space to issues that you care about will present valuable and rewarding opportunities.

> *The citizen statesperson is building community, engaging in and pulling together various stakeholders, and engendering conversations that can have a real impact.*

Of course, I'm still learning, still exploring, and still bringing people together. And that's something you can do, too.

Discussion Questions

- How have failures and successes in your life made you the person you are today?
- What goals would you like to achieve, and what are the first steps you will take to achieve them?
- How will you use these insights to drive impact in your community?

Appendix:
Additional Resources

Getting Started

Beginning your journey as a citizen statesperson can be daunting. We're here to tell you: you can do it. Use the following prompts to start on your path. We believe in you!

1. What are the causes that matter to you? Make a list of three to five issues that you see as important—in your local community, or around the world.
2. What expertise, experience, or even fresh perspectives do you bring to the topics you have identified? Even if you haven't worked in the areas previously, what insights can you share?
3. Who do you know working in the industry that interests you? Who knows more about the topic than you do? Write their names here. How could you contact these individuals (e.g., phone number, email address, LinkedIn, affiliation with a public organization)? As you move forward, keep a running list of relevant people in your network.
4. What public resources address your area of interest? Are there journals or news or media outlets that frequently discuss the topic? List the resources that can expand your knowledge and grow your expertise.
5. Once you have contacted the people in your immediate circle to discuss your interests, list your secondary contacts—that is, the people who you might not know personally, but who are recommended as authorities or active in your issue area. Put their names and contact information here, and then reach out to request a short conversation. You can use the following sample as a script to get you started:

Good morning, [name]. My name is [your name], and I'm [your relationship to a person they know]. I'm extremely interested in [issue area], and I'm looking for ways to become more involved in the issue. Your work in the area excites me. I would be grateful to learn from you and explore how I might be helpful. Would you be available for a very brief conversation in the coming weeks to discuss your work?

Sincerely,
[Your Name]

6. Established organizations and institutions are extremely useful for building contacts and expertise. What organizations focus on your issue area? Make a list of the most notable or respected organizations and identify individuals within those organizations whom you would like to contact. Include their names and contact information, if you can locate them. If you cannot locate contact information online, identify individuals through your LinkedIn network who could lead you to the target individuals. Pursue outreach!

7. Many organizations hold public events where you can meet and communicate with experts and leaders on a particular topic. Search the public calendars of the institutions and identified organizations and list relevant events over the next three months or calendar year. For each event you attend, take the name of at least one person you meet who can be a connection in the future.

8. You've had a chance to connect with knowledgeable individuals and experts on the topic that matters to you. What perspective haven't you been able to gain yet? What information do you need to fill the gaps in your knowledge? What people working on the ground have useful views? Record your thoughts and then look for ways to connect with those individuals to fill the gaps you identified.

Getting Involved

Now that you have begun putting together the initial building blocks of your work as a citizen statesperson, how can you use your experience and expertise to make an impact?

1. Start by charting a plan to guide your next steps. Write life goals with specific timelines for when you would like to accomplish your goals—short, medium, and longer term.
2. Identify opportunities for people who are interested in your issue area. What channels exist for you to gain hands-on experience, perhaps with a job or fellowship or in a volunteer role? Conduct research online and list ideas—and then apply for the opportunities! If your dream job or volunteer role does not exist, propose the idea by writing an email or scheduling a virtual meeting. We know for sure that the opportunity does not exist if you don't ask, so go ahead and ask! You don't know what's possible until you ask.
3. How can you get your name out into the world as someone who is interested in the issues that matter to you? Could you write an article or contribute a blog post? Could you plan an event or participate in a podcast? Record five specific ideas. Choose one idea and get started!
4. What places could you travel in order to become better informed or more connected around the issues you care about? Write down the names of those locations, and make plans to go there—either in person or virtually online.
5. If you need more ideas for ways to land a job or a fellowship or a volunteer opportunity in your area of interest, reach out to organizations, mentors, and advisors for ideas. Write three people you'll contact, and hold yourself accountable to contact them. Be sure to document the ideas they suggest, both for yourself and to demonstrate that you were listening carefully. Follow up with a thank you note and explore further their recommendations.
6. As you become more involved in the world of your chosen issue, people will look to you for leadership. What demonstrable changes will you make in your life to show your commitment to the cause? Start now!

Scaling

Once you have begun to make your mark in your issue area, you will want to find ways to broaden your influence. Use the following questions and exercises to plan your route forward.

1. What ways will you expand what you've learned to a bigger challenge or a larger stage? What places or communities face the issues you've begun to address in a more expansive or more dire way? How will you broaden your approach to make a more extensive impact?
2. Think about your mentors and advisors. Who can help you think through the best way to scale your work? List their names, and then contact these individuals to get their advice.
3. Consider the "Your Name, Inc." approach we described in the book. Think about what your dream organization looks like.
   o What is your overall mission?
   o What are your goals?
   o What is your competitive advantage?
   o Who is on your board of advisors?
4. Who are the other impactful people and organizations doing important work in your area of interest? Identify ways to partner on projects to expand your influence. Make a list of those individuals and organizations, and how to connect with them so that everyone is better because of the partnership.
5. How can you expand your leadership to others? Which prospective mentees and other rising leaders can help support and advise you? Record a few names, and then check in regularly to help them reach their potential.
6. Who can you help mentor now that you are scaling your leadership journey for greater social impact?

Fundraising Outlets for Social Entrepreneurs

The following list was inspired by a list formerly hosted at socialgoodguides.com.

Crowdfunding Platforms

- Angel List: angel.co
- CircleUp: circleup.com
- Crowdfunder: www.crowdfunder.com
- CrowdRise: www.crowdrise.com
- Funders Club: fundersclub.com
- Funding Circle: www.fundingcircle.com
- IndieGoGo: www.indiegogo.com
- Kickstarter: www.kickstarter.com
- Launcht: www.launcht.com
- Lending Club: www.lendingclub.com
- RocketHub: www.rockethub.com
- StartSomeGood: startsomegood.com
- SoMoLend: www.somolend.com
- WeFunder: www.wefunder.com

Accelerators

- Agora Partnerships: agora2030.org
- GoodCompany Ventures: goodcompanygroup.org
- Hub Ventures: hub-ventures.com
- Hult Prize: www.hultprize.org
- Impact Engine: www.theimpactengine.com
- Matter Media Entrepreneurship Accelerator: www.matter.vc
- Unreasonable Institute: www.uncharted.org
- VillageCapital: vilcap.com

Incubators

- Global Social Benefit Incubator: www.scu.edu/socialbenefit/entrepreneurship/gsbi

- Panzanzee: panzanzee.com
- Social Enterprise Greenhouse Incubator: segreenhouse.org/services/accelerate-your-enterprise/incubator
- Skoll Social Benefit Incubator: skollworldforum.org/gsbi/

Fellowships

- Global Good Fund: www.globalgoodfund.org
- Ashoka Fellows Program: usa.ashoka.org/nominate-ashoka-fellow
- Draper Richards Kaplan: www.drkfoundation.org
- Echoing Green: www.echoinggreen.org
- Eisenhower Fellowship: www.efworld.org/
- German Marshall Fund's Marshall Memorial Fellowship https:www.gmfus.org/marshall-memorial-fellowship
- Mentor Capital Network: www.mentorcapitalnet.org
- PopTech Social Innovation Fellows: www.poptech.com/sifellows
- Presidential Leadership Scholars: www.presidentialleadershipscholars.org/
- StartingBloc: startingbloc.org/about
- Schwab Foundation Fellows Program: www.schwabfound.org/content/selection-process

Pitch Competition

- Dell Social Innovation Challenge: www.dellchallenge.org

Foundations Doing Program-Related and/or Mission-Related Investing

- Aga Khan Foundation: www.akdn.org/akf
- Beyond Capital Fund: www.beyondcapitalfund.org
- Bill and Melinda Gates Foundation: www.gatesfoundation.org
- Blue Ridge Foundation: brfny.org
- Calvert Foundation: www.calvertfoundation.org
- Ford Foundation: www.fordfoundation.org

- Gates Family Foundation: www.gatesfamilyfoundation.org
- KL Felicitas Foundation: klfelicitasfoundation.org
- MacArthur Foundation: www.macfound.org
- Packard Foundation: www.packard.org
- Robert Wood Johnson Foundation: www.rwjf.org
- Root Capital: www.rootcapital.org
- W.K. Kellogg Foundation: www.wkkf.org

Sample Venture Philanthropy Funds

- Acumen Fund: www.acumen.org
- New Schools Venture Fund: www.newschools.org
- Omidyar Network: www.omidyar.com
- SV2 (Silicon Valley Social Venture Partners): www.sv2.org
- Social Venture Partners International: www.socialventure partners.org

Sample Angel Investors for Social Entrepreneurs

- Investors' Circle: www.investorscircle.net
- Pipeline Fellowship: www.pipelinefellowship.com
- Toniic: www.toniic.com

Databases of Angel Investors + Angel Groups

- Angel Capital Association: www.angelcapitalassociation.org
- Angel List: angel.co
- Gust: gust.com

Funds with Impact Focus

- Global Impact Fund II: https://globalgoodfund.org/about/ global-impact-fund-ii/
- City Light Capital: www.citylightcap.com
- DBL Investors: www.dblinvestors.com
- Gray Ghost Ventures: www.grayghostventures.com

- IGNIA: www.ignia.com.mx/bop
- Invested Development: investeddevelopment.com
- Kapor Capital: www.kaporcapital.com
- Renewal Funds: renewalfunds.com
- Unitus Impact: unituscapital.com

Grant Opportunities Database

- Candid (formerly known as the Foundation Center and Guidestar): https://candid.org/

About the Authors

Carrie Rich IS the co-founder and CEO of The Global Good Fund, a global nonprofit organization founded in 2013. At age 26, Ms. Rich felt privileged to have a mentor—the CEO of Inova Health System—who invested in her leadership as a young health administrator. Ms. Rich took this idea of pairing experienced business executives with emerging young social entrepreneurs to create a worldwide organization. Today, The Global Good Fund's cumulative impact includes 3,000 permanent jobs created in underserved communities, 200 entrepreneurs served in 40 countries, over 50,000 global community members, $150 million raised by the entrepreneurs, and nearly 10 million lives positively impacted.

In 2017, at age 29, Ms. Rich launched the Global Impact Fund, a venture capital fund that invests in socially impactful businesses. Eighty percent of the portfolio companies are led by Black, Brown, and women founders. Now on its second iteration, Global Impact Fund II continues to scale impact while creating wealth for a new league of investors—half of the Global Impact Fund II investor base is Black, Brown, and women.

Fundamentally, Ms. Rich's message is about accessibility, how everyday people can empower themselves and others. That is why Ms. Rich is active in her local community serving as a volunteer. Ms. Rich volunteers monthly with her young children to teach them the value of giving back through activities like packing food for low-income children in Baltimore, picking up trash near the nature center, and joining others to serve Christmas dinner alongside the nuns at Gift of Peace convent in Washington, D.C.

Ms. Rich serves on the board of directors of Trinity Health System and the Atlas Health Foundation. She is on the Dean's Advisory Council for the College of Health at Lehigh University. During Ms. Rich's time as a student at Lehigh University, she penned a letter to the president of the university, making the case for a health-focused interdisciplinary program, which is now one of the most popular majors at the university.

Ms. Rich attended Georgetown University for her master's in health systems administration and obtained a certificate in healthcare quality from Harvard University. She is the author of three books: *Health Entrepreneurship: A Practical Guide*, and two editions of *Sustainability for Healthcare Management: A Leadership Imperative*, which became a top five business book in *Handelsblatt* (Germany). Ms. Rich taught nursing students at Georgetown University and George Washington University, and currently teaches "Fundraising for Social Impact" to a global audience at the Amani Institute. She is the recipient of the *Daily Record*'s Most Admired CEO, the EY Entrepreneur of the Year award, and POLITICO Women Who Rule award.

Ms. Rich lives with her husband and three young children in Maryland, where they enjoy spending time together as a family in the countryside.

Dean Fealk is an award-winning international attorney and civic leader bridging sectors to partner alongside business, government, and NGOs to promote international security, democracy, and shared prosperity. As Northern California Co-Managing Partner of a leading global law firm, he advises multinational companies on key strategic and legal issues related to growing their business internationally, having counseled on more than US$40 billion in cross-border transactions.

Dean also serves in leadership capacities to various civic organizations, including CEO business groups, NGOs, and think tanks, and has advised and convened government leaders and politicians around the world—from the NATO secretary general to the mayor of Seoul to the justice minister of India—on international public policy issues. He is a co-founding member of the Halifax International Security Forum, the premier nonprofit organization dedicated to strengthening strategic cooperation among democratic nations. Dean is also co-founder of Transatlantic West, a community of leaders promoting stronger ties between Europe and Silicon Valley.

Passionate about service and public policy, Dean has advised three presidential campaigns on foreign policy and represented the State of California in trade and investment missions around the world. He serves as a governor's appointee on the California Workforce Development Board, promoting job quality, worker voice, equity, and environmental sustainability for the state's 18 million workers. He is past chair of the Northern California District Export Council, appointed by the U.S. secretary of commerce to represent and advocate on behalf of the region's diverse array of exporters, resulting in $75 billion in annual exports. He has also advised the U.S. trade representative on international trade issues impacting the technology and innovation ecosystem.

Recognized for his leadership in public diplomacy, Dean has been designated an Honorary Senator of the German Economy, an Eisenhower Fellow to China, a Presidential Leadership Scholar, a Marshall Memorial Fellow to the EU, a U.S.–Spain Council Young Leader, an International Fellow of the Center for Strategic International Studies, a Truman National Security Fellow, and a Carnegie New Leader. He is a life member of the Council on Foreign Relations.

Dean began his career in East Asia, where he practiced law, consulted for the World Bank, and, as a Fulbright Scholar, served as the first American to clerk at the Constitutional Court of Korea. He is a graduate of the London School of Economics, the University of California, Leadership San Francisco, and Harvard Business School's Executive Leadership Program.

Dean lives with his wife, daughter, and son in Piedmont, California.

Index